Jerome L. Stein (Ed.)

The Globalization of Markets

Capital Flows, Exchange Rates and Trade Regimes

With 13 Figures

Physica-Verlag

A Springer-Verlag Company

Prof. Dr. Jerome L. Stein
Departments of Economics, Applied Mathematics
Brown University
Providence
Rhode Island 02912, USA

First published in "Economic Systems merged with JOICE"
Volume 20, Issue 2/3 1996

ISBN 3-7908-0965-9 Physica-Verlag Heidelberg

Die Deutsche Bibliothek – CIP-Einheitsaufnahme
The globalization of markets: capital flows, exchange rates and trade regimes / Jerome
L. Stein (ed.). – Heidelberg: Physica-Verl., 1997
   Aus: Economic systems merged with JOICE; Vol. 20, 1996
   ISBN 3-7908-0965-9
NE: Stein, Jerome L. [Hrsg.]

© Physica-Verlag Heidelberg 1997
Printed in Germany

The use of general descriptive names, registered names, trademarks, etc. in this publica-
tion does not imply, even in the absence of a specific statement, that such names are
exempt from the relevant protective laws and regulations and therefore free for general
use.

SPIN 10547965   88/2202-5 4 3 2 1 0 – Printed on acid-free paper

Preface

The interrelated issues analyzed in this book are as follows. With the integration of Europe, there are free movements in goods, services, short and long term capital, and direct investment. The German mark is the key currency in Europe and its value will affect the equilibrium bilateral exchange rates of the other currencies in the European Union. It is important to examine the following issues. What have been the fundamental determinants of the real value of the mark since the period of floating? What will be the effects of German integration upon exchange rates? How can we measure whether currencies are misaligned or if exchange rates are at their equilibrium values? Are short term capital flows destabilizing and, if so, should they be discouraged through a transactions tax? Under what conditions does the formation of a regional trading bloc help or hinder the liberalization of world trade? What are the determinants of foreign direct investment made by multinational enterprises?

There is a unity to this book. The authors are senior scholars who approach the subject from the theoretical, policy oriented and econometric points of view.

Jerome L. Stein

Contents

A Currency Transactions Tax. Why and How

JAMES TOBIN

Cowles Foundation for Research in Economics, Yale University, P.O. Box 208281, New Haven, Connecticut 06520-8281

Abstract

The traditional controversy between "fixed" and "floating" exchange rate regimes is obsolete. Both are vulnerable to capital movements across currencies. Transactions taxes create room for needed differences in domestic macroeconomic policies.

I proposed a uniform worldwide tax on spot transactions across currencies in 1978 in my presidential address to the Eastern Economics Association. I have written and spoken on the proposal several times since, but I'm not the type to wage ardent crusades for my crackpot ideas – unlike my great predecessor at Yale, Irving Fisher. I warned the organizers of this conference that I don't have anything significant new to say on the subject.

When foreign exchanges seem to be messing up monetary and economic affairs in the ways that seemed to me in 1978 to be inevitable, my proposal gets discovered or rediscovered. Recently it has been discovered by a non-economics constituency, those looking for ways to finance the United Nations and other international agencies when the demands upon them are exploding and the member nations are stingy in supporting them.

Flexible or adjustable currency exchange rates plus free movement of funds across currencies are a compound hazardous to the economic health of nations. So say both logic and experience. One way out, of course, is to make exchange rates inflexible and unadjustable – irrevocably fixed, as is true within the United States or Canada or the United Kingdom or other federations, and as may eventually be true within the European Union. However, as the slow and rocky road to Maastricht repeatedly shows, permanent currency unification requires economic,

---

[1] This paper uses in part materials in "Two Arguments for Sand in the Wheels of International Finance," by Barry Eichengreen, James Tobin, and Charles Wyplosz, *Economic Journal,* January 1995, pp. 162–171.

political, and social convergences well beyond those achieved in the decades since the Treaty of Rome. Extensions of currency unification to all of Europe, to the whole Group of Seven, to the emerging industrial economies of Asia, to the whole world, are many decades more distant.

For a long time ahead, we are stuck with national currencies, trying to find the best way to live with them. Yet vast funds are prepared to arbitrage away differences in national interest rates and to speculate on exchange rates. Here, as in many other dimensions of life on this globe, technologies have outrun economic, political, and social institutions. It is important to make distinct national currencies tolerable, and to make international money and capital markets compatible with modest national autonomy in monetary and macroeconomic policy. That is the economic motivation for proposals to throw some "sand in the wheels" of the over-efficient international financial vehicles.

This is, in a sense, a move backward, towards the exchange and capital controls that made past international regimes workable. But it is important not to restore the hodge-podge of nationalistic and bureaucratic controls of those days. Instead, let us seek an internationally agreed, symmetrical, and neutral way to slow down international financial flows, and one with minimal deterrence of trade in goods and services and minimal interference with efficient allocation of real capital among nations.

The traditional controversy between "fixed" and "floating" exchange rate regimes is obsolete. Both regimes are vulnerable to capital movements across currencies. Both involve changeable exchange rates and invite transactions to profit from interest differentials and exchange rate movements. In a floating rate regime, those movements occur in markets, overwhelmingly as a result of private transactions, though sometimes with official currency interventions as well. In a fixed rate regime, changes in the parities which national governments and central banks are committed to maintain involve deliberate official decisions, usually forced by a government's inability to fulfill earlier solemn commitments.

Speculation on currencies occurs in both regimes. Nostalgia for the pre-1971 Bretton Woods system or for a full-fledged gold standard reflects a "grass is greener" syndrome rather than thoughtful analysis. In those fixed-rate regimes, currency parities could be changed and were changed. In their best years these regimes benefitted from circumstances that do not now obtain. First, they were managed by a dominant country with sufficient international financial clout to make its own currency invulnerable, the pre-1914 gold standard by Great Britain, the 1946–1966 Bretton Woods system by the United States. Second, the other national members of the system could and did protect their currencies by exchange regulations and capital controls. Anyway, private funds ready to speculate on currencies were much less formidable threats than they have become now that they greatly exceed central banks' reserves. Third, voters were more tolerant of the economic costs of maintaining over-valued exchange rates. Nowadays governments are held much more responsible for macroeconomic outcomes than before the Second World War or even in the early postwar years.

The crises and defections that afflicted the European Monetary System in 1992–93 are convincing recent demonstrations that adjustable pegs are not viable. Consequently, serious advocates of official parities have been moving towards market flexibility by widening substantially the bands of permissible deviations from parities, and by smoothing-formulas for automatic adjustment of the central parities themselves towards market experience. Even so, these parameters of the system, the central parities and the limits of the bands, remain vulnerable to speculative attack whenever it appears that the risks of official change in them are predominantly in one direction. Wide bands did not prevent exchange crises in Europe in recent years, or in Mexico in winter 1994–95.

At the same time, experience since 1971 has not fulfilled the more extreme claims of the advocates of floating rates. They thought that exchange rates could be left wholly to private markets, that official neglect of them would be unambiguously benign, indeed optimal. Governments, it turned out, could not be indifferent to currency markets. Volatility in exchange rates and interest rates induced by speculation and capital flows could have real economic consequences devastating for particular sectors and whole economies. For example, the surprise appreciation of the U.S. dollar against the Japanese yen in the early 1980s nearly destroyed the American automotive industry.

Advocates of floating rates had argued that they would free national monetary policies from constraints imposed by commitments to defend official parities. But the same interest arbitrage that limits the autonomy of a central bank in a fixed-exchange-rate regime restricts its powers in a floating-rate regime. If similar financial assets denominated in two different currencies are perfect substitutes in private portfolios, they cannot bear different interest returns in their domestic currencies unless those differences are offset by expected exchange rate movements. Central banks and governments cannot create exchange rate expectations consistent with the domestic interest rates they desire. It is true that exchange market volatility itself should make assets in different currencies imperfect substitutes and create a bit of room for independent monetary policies. But the swings in pervasive market sentiment that generate much of the volatility are not helpful.

Globalization of financial markets has been a much heralded achievement. Innovations in technologies of computation and communications, new markets and institutions, and tides of deregulation have released a flood of domestic and international financial transactions. Vast resources of human intelligence are engaged. Evidently gross foreign exchange transactions alone amount to a trillion dollars daily. Economies of scale are enormous. Transaction costs are small and virtually independent of the amount transacted. Arbitrage or speculative transactions in foreign exchange are so large that minuscule percentages of price spell enormous gains or losses on the capital at stake. The outcomes of financial markets impinge on real economies, local, national, and international, where adjustments are sluggish, transactions are costly, transportation is slow and expensive, substitutions are imperfect and time-consuming, and expectations are fuzzy.

Transactions taxes are one way, a quite innocuous way, to throw some sand in the wheels of super-efficient financial vehicles. A half percent tax translates into an annual rate of four percent on a three months' round trip into a foreign money market, more for shorter round trips. It is this effect that creates room for differences in domestic interest rates, allowing national monetary policies to respond to domestic macroeconomic needs. The same tax would be smaller deterrent to slower round trips. It would be a negligible consideration in long-term portfolio or direct investments in other economies. It would be too small, relative to ordinary commercial and transportation costs, to have much effect on commodity trade.

J. M. Keynes pointed out in 1936 that a transactions tax could strengthen the weight of long-range fundamentals in stock-market pricing, as against speculators' guesses of the short-range behaviors of other speculators. The same applies to bond markets and to foreign exchange markets. Recently speculators in all these financial markets have focussed on particular items of news, especially on macroeconomic events, statistics, and policies. Keynes's beauty contest applies: speculators concentrate on how "the markets" will respond to news, not on basic economic meanings and portents.

The hope that transactions taxes would diminish excess volatility depends on the likelihood that Keynes's speculators have shorter horizons and holding periods than market participants oriented to long-range fundamentals. If so, it is speculators who are the more deterred by the tax. But it is true that some stabilizing transactions might also be discouraged; fundamentalists alert to long-run opportunities created by speculative vagaries would have to pay the tax too. The judgment that those benign influences are not now dominant in short runs is based on a presumption that the markets would not be so volatile if they were.

In any case, the principal purpose of the proposed tax is to expand the autonomy of national monetary policies. That does not depend on the success of the tax in reducing volatility. The tax would not, of course, permit national macroeconomic authorities to ignore the international repercussions of their policies. In particular, the tax could not protect patent misvaluations in exchange parities; speculators' gains from betting on inevitable near-term realignments would far exceed the tax costs. Nor would the tax make macroeconomic policy coordination among major governments unnecessary or undesirable. The G-7 ought to concern itself, more than it does now, with the world-wide average level and trend of interest rates, from which individual nations should deviate in accordance up and down with their circumstances.

Vast resources of intelligence and enterprise are wasted in financial speculation, largely in playing zero-sum games. Transactions taxes might reallocate some of these resources. To the extent that they do not, they would at least collect needed public revenues for under-supported international purposes, without the bad side effects of conventional taxes. [I have no estimate of the potential revenues. The yield of a 0.5% tax on a base of a trillion dollars a day is 1.75 trillion a year. But I assume that the trillion per day is mostly derivative transactions, while the tax applies to spot exchanges.]

In my original article proposing the tax, I advocated channeling the monies collected by the tax to international purposes. I mentioned in particular the World Bank, thinking of subsidizing loans to poor developing countries. Now, however, there is a growing constituency of advocates of the tax for its revenue-raising potential, not its incentive effects. There is always a tradeoff between these two goals. The more the tax succeeds in the economic objectives that primarily motivated me, and the handful of economists who agree with me, the less revenues it collects for worldwide good works. In this case, however, there's plenty for both. Certainly the needs for resources for international purposes have exploded, as multilateral peacemaking and peacekeeping forces are in great demand, and refugees are suffering all over the world.

A foreign exchange transactions tax would apply to all spot exchanges of currencies. Although collected by the jurisdictions where exchanges occur, the tax would have to be internationally uniform, universal enough to render infeasible any important tax-saving relocations of exchange markets. Enforcement would depend principally on the major banks of the world and on the jurisdictions that regulate them. Exchanges between closely related currencies could be exempted on application from the governments involved to the international administrator of the system.

To begin with, an international conference, a mini Bretton Woods, would have to negotiate an agreement establishing the system. The international administrator might logically be the International Monetary Fund. Or a new international financial agency responsible to the member nations might be set up for the purpose, assisted by the IMF and possibly also the Bank for International Settlements. The administrator might be given discretion to set the size of the tax within limits. The administrator would assure the uniformity of the tax among jurisdictions and would handle the transfers of the agreed shares of revenues to the designated international institutions. Exemptions from the tax for linked currencies would have to be adjudicated. The rate of tax might need to be changed from time to time. The IMF, bereft of its original central functions by the demise of the Bretton Woods monetary system and superseded by regional regimes in Europe, should welcome these new responsibilities.

Critics of the "Tobin tax" are sure that transactions would be moved from financial centers to "off-shore" tax-free locations. I suspect that this danger is exaggerated. There are considerable costs, both fixed and operating, involved in such relocations. Otherwise low wages and rent would already have have offered opportunities for saving brokerage costs and existing taxes and attracted many more financial activities, markets, and institutions than they have.

Nevertheless, it is certainly desirable to assure that all jurisdictions cooperate. Therefore, I propose that collection of the tax be required of every member of the IMF, as a condition of eligibility for credit from the Fund. As a result, "outlaws" not cooperating with the international tax would probably have difficulties getting credit or assistance anywhere.

Most, but not all, of the aggregate revenues collected by the national jurisdictions would be dedicated to international purposes and turned over to international institutions. But the formula for splitting revenues would be progressive. Poor and small countries would keep for themselves most or all of the revenues they collect. The purpose of requiring their adherence is to prevent them from undermining the system by not participating, not to collect major revenues when they do participate. The big financial powers would be the big sources of revenue for international purposes.

Other criticisms of the currency transactions tax are variations on the theme that markets generate optimal results, so that this interference in them is bound to be bad. There's no arguing with true believers in the faith. Given the myriad other hurdles to real commercial and capital transactions in the world, it's hard to see how this modes tax can result in noticeable distortions. Indeed if it yields exchange rates that better reflect long-run fundamentals, it will enhance welfare.

Some critics do not sympathize with my objective of preserving a modicum of autonomy for national monetary policies. They regard any discipline that currency arbitrage and speculation imposes on any country as justified. Let all countries avoid demand-management policies, both monetary and fiscal, and we will all converge to our natural rates of unemployment. I think the experience of Europe over the last fifteen years refutes that Panglossian view. The theory on which it is based is mostly a product of American economists, but fortunately neither our government nor (at least to date) our central bank has taken it as seriously as European policy-makers. I cannot expect those who diverge so basically from my macroeconomic premises to see any good in my proposal.

Finally, of course, I cannot expect bankers and others who would pay the tax, or suffer any reduction it might cause in the transactions from which they profit, to approve. They, of course, have considerable influence on central bankers and on international monetary and financial officials.

Discussant to Professor J. Tobin

CHARLES A. GOODHART

The London School of Economics and Political Science,
Houghton Street, London WC2A 2AE, England

Abstract

While I do not accept in full the cynicism and distrust of governments of the public choice school,
I feel that Tobin's claim: that the tax would allow national monetary policies to respond to
domestic macroeconomic needs, does seem to come out of the older representation of
government as selflessly and efficiently maximising public welfare.

The only reason that I can imagine why I was asked to be a discussant of Professor
Tobin's paper is that I am probably one of the few present who has actually paid a
Tobin transaction tax.

It may not be quite exactly what he has advocated, but every bank transfer in
Brazil has incurred recently an ad valorem tax of 1/4 of 1 per cent. And when I was
taken to draw out some reals to meet my local expenses at a Conference in Sao
Paulo in September, 1994, an amount of 290 reals, I paid my tax of 0.72 reals. I even
kept my tax receipt to give to him.

I have to tell him that the imposition of this tax involves some considerable
deadweight costs. I had to stand in line several minutes longer, and even the time
and effort of writing out the tax form by the bank clerk cost more than the pittance
paid over. The tax was initially imposed as a single year crisis measure, and is not
much enjoyed by anyone, locals or non-residents.

At a time when the costs of making relatively small retail type trans-European
bank transfers have come in for extremely bad publicity, and are widely regarded
as representing a serious obstacle for small and medium companies entering into
European trade outside their own countries, the idea of actually consciously
adding to such costs seems somewhat bizarre.

Let me start, therefore, by making Professor Tobin a suggestion for improving
his proposal, which is that he exempts all spot exchange transactions under some
ceiling from the tax, say any transaction below ecu 10,000. But you will, no doubt,
say that that opens up a loophole whereby a speculator can simply split his deals
into myriad small deals. To that I would have two answers. First, as I shall try to
demonstrate shortly, this loophole is only one among many others, and far from

the biggest. My second point is that even in an age of automation and computers there do remain fixed costs connected with registering, processing and accounting for separate transactions, and if a speculator is forced into 1000 transactions, rather than 1 transaction in order to take a speculative position of 10 mn ecu, it will make a considerable difference to his overall costs.

Let me turn next to some of the loopholes. Professor Tobin implies in his paper that the tax would apply only to spot exchange transactions and not to derivatives. But speculators will be just as happy to use the wide range of possibilities opened up by derivatives in order to take up a speculative position. Shortly before this Conference, I was reading a paper by Robert Merton in which he criticized margining regulations in the NYSE on the grounds that there were at least nine other ways to take a levered position in the S & P 500 stocks besides buying on margin in the cash market. Let me quote Garber and Taylor's Economic Journal forum paper (1995) which will accompany Tobin's,

> "If foreign exchange is defined as an exchange of one bank deposit for another in a different currency, gross trading in these claims will be effectively eliminated in favour of T-bill swaps in currencies with liquid (same day) T-bill markets. The swapped T-bills will be immediately sold for deposits. The foreign exchange market will shift to this form, no tax will be paid, and position taking will be unaffected.
>
> If supervisors have the sophistication to see through this subterfuge and begin taxing T-bill transactions, other methods can be employed. For example, certain combinations of stock market baskets and index options are equivalent to cash according to options pricing theory. Such combinations in one country can be swapped for similar combinations in another country – this is a foreign exchange equivalent. Again, to control this operation, the tax would have to be extended out of straight foreign exchange to transactions in an ever-widening ring of securities and derivatives markets."

There are, indeed, (n) alternative ways through which a speculator can go long or short of a currency without going himself through the spot market, and n is quite a large number, probably over 5. But the derivatives markets are linked to the cash, spot market, and a speculation in the futures, options or swap market will be translated via arbitrage or hedging to the spot market. The simplest case is arbitrage between the futures and the spot market. Much, probably most, of such arbitrage and hedging foreign exchange in the market is undertaken by banks. One question that I had for Professor Tobin is whether he intended purely *interbank* spot transactions to bear his tax.

Let me propose to him that purely interbank deals *must* also bear his transaction tax, for at least three reasons.

(1) Otherwise speculators would use the derivative market and banks would transmit the effect to the spot market. The result would be that the tax would be totally bypassed.

(2) Some of the main speculators, at least on a very short-term intraday basis, have probably been the banks themselves.
(3) The definition of a bank is somewhat porous, and were banks excluded from the ambit of the tax, one could imagine the mushroom growth of name-plate banks in various Caribbean tax havens whose function would be to facilitate speculation.

[At the Conference Professor Tobin confirmed that in his plan interbank deals would be as much subject to the tax as any other spot transaction.]

Once banks *are* included within the ambit of the tax, one then has to recognize that any non-bank final customer forex order generates a subsequent chain of interbank deals, the hot potato hypothesis, whereby a non-bank order induces a whole series of subsequent bank portfolio inventory rebalancing (Lyons 1994). The $ trillion a day figure which Tobin quotes is widely believed to be mostly made up of interbank deals. So, if interbank deals are included, an initial client order will generate a multiple number of forex transactions, each of which would be taxed.

This has its good and its bad sides. The banks would no doubt seek to defray the extra costs of dealing by widening their bid ask spread. So after taking account of this, the overall tax rate that Tobin would need to impose to deter speculation would be a fraction, perhaps a quarter or fifth of the size that he currently puts forward. The bad aspects are, of course, that no one knows what the multiple involved in rebalancing interbank transactions actually is, and also that the sharply widening spreads would make the market thinner, more expensive and at any rate in the very short run more volatile than now.

There are, indeed, a whole host of practical problems that would be involved in trying to levy this tax, some of which Tobin fully recognizes, such as the need to apply it in all major centres in a uniform way. I have touched on certain other potential loopholes. Frankly, I think that, in the absence of quite comprehensive exchange controls, such a tax would almost certainly be avoided and evaded by those on whom it was meant to bear, and that the dead weight costs would fall instead on tourists and those involved in foreign trade, at least unless my suggestion of exempting all small transactions were accepted. [Professor Tobin expressed a willingness to do so at the Conference.]

However, I now want to turn away from consideration of the practicality of such a tax, to the purpose of the tax. Here I shall abstract both from the question of the good works that might be financed from the tax receipts and the extra impetus that it would provide for EMU. The main purpose for the tax in Tobin's presentation, because the claim is made several times, is that it would provide some additional modest autonomy to national monetary policy makers. Now I understand that argument in the context of pegged but adjustable rate systems with narrow bands, as the old ERM was. Yet it seems that Tobin does not believe that the sand, or frictions, created by his scheme either could, or should, (I am not quite certain which) allow for the restoration of a narrow band ERM system. Thus he notes that 1992/93 provided "convincing demonstrations that adjustable pegs are not viable". And he notes that "speculators' gains from betting on inevitable near-term realignments would far exceed the tax cost."

So his purpose is not to resurrect the old Delors plan of transition into EMU via ever tighter parities, a transition plan that I hope we would all agree had been demonstrated to be neither necessary nor optimal for a move to EMU. Instead, he seems to see this tax as a beneficial accompaniment not only for a much wider band regime but even for floating. Tobin stresses that, even in the context of a free float, national monetary authorities in the present global financial market have lost a lot of their autonomy.

Here I cannot go along with his analysis. On a purely empirical basis, apart from our period in, and earlier when shadowing, the ERM, I cannot recall an occasion, (apart perhaps from the early 1980s), when an interest rate change in the UK that was deemed desirable on domestic grounds was aborted, prevented or subsequently reversed by external influences. Tobin's analytical argument is, I think, a variant of the Dornbusch model, whereby the forward exchange rate is anchored by expectations about fundamentals, so that the spot rate has to jump in response to interest rate shifts. That model was indeed elegant, but unfortunately wrong. Exactly those speculators prepared to bet on fundamentals are the ones that Tobin himself notes are *not* present to prevent longer term misalignments and to help stabilize the system. The forward-rate is *not* the best expectation of the future spot rate and uncovered interest parity does not hold. While national interest rate changes undoubtedly do affect their exchange rates, there is no evidence that such effects are so large or destabilising within a freely floating system that they seriously preclude national monetary autonomy.

Moreover, if such effects of domestic monetary policies on exchange rates were further attenuated from what they are now, I would not regard that as an uncovenanted benefit either. Market reactions in the forex market, as in the bond market, reveal the market's assessment of such policy. Now such assessments can be wrong or biassed, the thermometer can give mistaken readings, but trying to suppress the fluctuation of the mercury in the thermometer because it is from time to time misleading is not necessarily the best policy.

While I do not accept, at any rate in full, the deep cynicism and distrust of governments of the public choice school, I do feel that Tobin's claim that the tax would 'allow national monetary policies to respond to domestic macroeconomic needs' does seem to come straight out of the older representation of government as selflessly and efficiently maximising public welfare, a view the public choice school criticized so severely. Thus the cynics amongst us would say that Tobin's frictions would more often be utilised to hold domestic real interest rates down, at the expense of worse potential future inflation. I do not think that I want to remove the feet of government from being held to the fire of continuous market examination, imperfect though the latter is. So, even if Tobin's tax could be made a practical possibility, which I doubt, I would not favour its introduction.

References

Eichengreen B, Tobin J, Wyplosz C (1995) Two Cases for Sand in the Wheels of International Finance. Economic Journal 105 (428):162–172

Garber P, Taylor M (1995) Sand in the Wheels of Foreign Exchange Markets: A Skeptical Note. Economic Journal 105 (428):173–180

Lyons R (1994) Foreign exchange volume: Sound and fury signifying nothing, paper presented at the NBER Conference on "Microstructure of foreign exchange markets", Perugia, Italy, proceedings forthcoming, eds Frankel J, Galli G, Giovannini A

The Equilibrium Real Exchange Rate of Germany

JEROME L. STEIN

Department of Economics, Brown University, Providence RI 02912, USA.
FAX (401) 863–1970, E-mail JLS@BROWNVM.BROWN.EDU

KARLHANS SAUERNHEIMER

Johannes Gutenberg Universität, Mainz, Germany. FAX 49/6131/39-5527

Abstract

The NATREX model defines the fundamental determinants of the equilibrium real effective exchange rate in the medium to longer run. The PPP theory is a special case of the NATREX when a linear combination of the fundamentals, which are productivity and social thrift, is stationary. The differences in social thrift under Schmidt and Kohl, and the effects of the European terms of trade upon the q-ratio, explain the variations in the NATREX in the preunification period. The actual real exchange rate of the German mark converged to the NATREX. In the postunification period, the medium run NATREX increased due to the rise in time preference and the cyclically adjusted q-ratio. The actual real exchange rate appreciated accordingly. However, the rise in time preference has lowered the longer run value of the NATREX.

Objectives

For very open economies like the Federal Republic of Germany the real effective exchange rate is an economic variable of major importance. The effects of the exchange rate upon an economy are positively related to the degree of openess of an economy. Germany is an extremely open economy. In 1992 the ratio of exports plus imports to GDP was 46% compared to 16% in Japan and 17% in the US[1]. Furthermore, Germany is deeply integrated into the international financial markets. There is complete freedom of capital movements and the DM is a reserve currency second in the world after the US dollar. The strong dependence of the German economy on the international markets for goods and financial assets has induced the economic policymakers in Germany to give a high priority to exchange rate issues.

There is general agreement that exchange rates should reflect economic fundamentals and that excess volatility is undesirable. The questions that we address in this paper are to what extent have the variations in the German real effective exchange rate been the result of variations in the fundamentals at home

---

[1] International Monetary Fund, International Financial Statistics.

and abroad, and to what extent are they due to short term transitory factors or misapprehension by the market concerning what are the fundamentals which determine the sustainable real exchange rates? To answer these questions, we must have a benchmark of what is the equilibrium or sustainable real exchange rate generated by the fundamentals. We must understand what is a correct model of real exchange rates, what are the fundamentals and what is an equilibrium or sustainable exchange rate.

The real value of the German mark is also important for the viability of the European Monetary System (EMS) with fixed exchange rates. From 1987 to the autumn of 1992, nominal exchange rates in the EMS remained unchanged despite divergent rates of inflation. There were currency crises in the autumn of 1992 and summer of 1993. The resulting capital flights forced the governments to realign their currencies. The new parities agreed upon in September 1992 proved not to be sustainable and on September 16 and 17, 1992 the British pound and Italian lira left the exchange rate mechanism. On August 2, 1993, after further speculative attacks, especially against the French franc, the EC finance ministers and central bank governors decided to enlarge temporarily the bands for the bilateral exchange rates from $\pm 2.25\%$ to $\pm 15\%$. The major question for the European Union is whether the exchange rates will stabilize near the existing parity.

The German unification was a political event which has economic consequences for the equilibrium real exchange rate. Insofar as the unification leads to a significant appreciation of the equilibrium real exchange rate then there are several possibilities. Either the nominal value of German mark must appreciate relative to the EMS currencies or German prices must rise relative to the prices in the other EC countries. If the German Bundesbank follows its traditional anti-inflationary policies, then the prices in the other EMS countries must decline. With nominal wage stickiness, there would be adverse medium run effects upon employment in the other countries. It is therefore important to evaluate the magnitude of the effects of the German unification upon the equilibrium German real exchange rate.

To answer the above questions it is necessary to have a model which explains what factors determine the moving equilibrium real exchange rate of a currency. A distinction is made between the fundamentals which determine the trend movements of the real exchange rate and the transitory factors which produce noisy variations around the moving equilibrium real exchange rate.

We proceed as follows. First, we present the most important stylized facts relevant to our analysis. The contemporary models are unable to explain these stylized facts and hence cannot serve as explanations of the determinants of the real exchange rate. That is why we use our Natural Real Exchange Rate (NATREX) model. Second, we explicitly develop the structural equations of our model, which is more general and flexible than the contemporary models. We explain, within the context this theoretically consistent growth model, what are the fundamental external and domestic determinants of the real effective exchange rate of Germany. The fundamentals are time preference measured as the ratio of social consumption to GDP and the productivity of capital reflected in the Keynes-Tobin q-ratio. The variables which help determine the q-ratio are the European terms of trade and the rate of capacity utilization. Fourth, we show that the long run effects of the fundamentals estimated in our cointegrating equations are consistent with the movements in the real exchange rate predicted by the model.

There are several concepts of the real exchange rate. The real exchange rate that we focus upon is the real effective exchange rate as reported in the International Monetary Fund's International Financial Statistics[2]. It is the ratio of domestic to foreign normalized unit labor costs in a common currency. The weighting scheme used to construct the rates is based upon disaggregated data for trade among the seventeen industrial countries in manufactured goods for 1980. The weights reflect the relative importance of both a country's trading partners in its direct bilateral trade relations and competition in third markets. Normalized unit labor costs in manufacturing (w, w') are calculated by dividing an index of actual hourly compensation per worker (W, W') by a five-year moving average index of output per manhour (A, A'). We may express the real effective exchange rate R as equation (1). Foreign variables are denoted with a prime. The nominal effective exchange rate is denoted by N, where a rise in N or R signifies an appreciation.

$$R = N\, w/w' = (NW/A)/(W'/A') \tag{1}$$

The real value of the German mark converges to the NATREX, which is our moving equilibrium. The unexplained deviation between the real value of the mark and the NATREX averages out to zero but has a high variance. The Purchasing Power Parity PPP is a special case of the NATREX, when the NATREX is stationary. The equilibrium nominal rate is the NATREX times the ratio of foreign to domestic prices. The reason why PPP theory is not valid[3] is that the equilibrium real exchange rate inherits the characteristics of the fundamentals. If a linear combination of the fundamentals is stationary, then so also will be the NATREX; and the PPP theory would be valid. This has not been the case during the floating rate period.

Our approach is positive, not normative. We do not suggest that the derived equilibrium rate is desirable[4]. We do not advocate that the nominal rate should be managed or that domestic policies should be changed to produce a given real

---

[2] The data, which come from the International Financial Statistics IFS, are denoted by a country prefix GR for Germany and a suffix which is the row in the IFS. Thus the real effective exchange rate for Germany is GRREU and the nominal effective exchange rate is GRNEU.

[3] See Breuer for a critique of the recent empirical studies of PPP

[4] The NATREX differs from the Fundamental Equilibrium Real Exchange Rate (FEER) of Williamson and the Desired Equilibrium Exchange rate (DEER) of Bayoumi et al., which are normative concepts. See Clark (in this issue) for an analysis of the relations among these three concepts.

exchange rate. We take the sum of public plus private consumption/GDP as an exogenous fundamental, which we call the social time preference rate. We show the effects of variation in the time preference ratio upon the trajectory of the equilibrium exchange rate and the evolution of the external debt. The sustainable equilibrium value of the debt is positively related to the social rate of time preference. Our equilibrium debt is sustainable but, unlike Williamson who has a normative concept in mind, we do not discuss whether the social time preference ratio and resulting steady state debt are desirable.

Stylized Facts

There has been a succession of models which have attempted to explain the large exchange rate movements observed in the post 1973 period.[5] By now there is overwhelming evidence that the standard models are not able to explain exchange rate movements among the G7 countries. After stating the stylized facts [SF] we indicate why these models are unable to explain exchange rate variations, and will justify why we take a more general and less restrictive approach. Many of these facts concern the stationarity of series. A series is defined as weakly stationary if it reverts to a constant mean.[6] All of the data are from the IMF, International Financial Statistics, quarterly, 1973.1-1994.1 except where otherwise noted.

The first set of contemporary models are based upon monetary dynamics with rational expectations. These models were attractive because they implied an overshooting hypothesis such that there could be large exchange rate variations in a world of rational expectations. The large variations are produced by rationally expected monetary policies. These models are not valid for Germany because they are inconsistent with stylized facts [SF1] [SF2] [SF3] described below.

[SF1]   The real effective exchange rate of Germany is not stationary. The mean is not independent of time. The real effective (GRREU) and nominal effective (GRNEU) exchange rates move together in the longer run, as shown in figure 1.

---

[5] The Mundell-Fleming model was replaced the portfolio models which then were followed by the monetary theories of the balance of payments which gave way to Dornbusch's model which was succeeded by the representative agent-intertemporal optimization models. The moral is that one should have some humility in presenting a model and not to claim that his model is correct because it is based upon "optimization" and the other models are "ad hoc", which means "It is not my model".

[6] A stationary series has a finite mean and variance both of which are independent of time. If the mean varies with time, it is not stationary. The stationary results are based upon the Dickey-Fuller (DF) or adjusted Dickey-Fuller statistics (ADF).

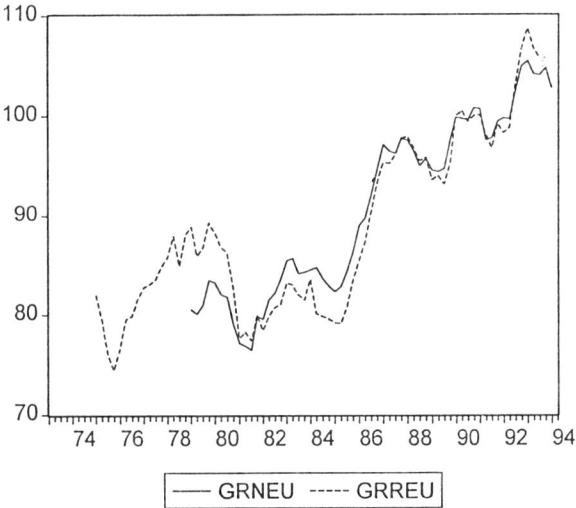

Fig. 1. German real effective exchange rate (GRREU), nominal effective exchange rate (GRNEU).

[SF2]   The nominal DM/$ is not positively related to, or cointegrated with, the ratio of German/US money stocks per unit of output[7]. This is seen in figure 2 where DM/$US, denoted DMUS, is plotted on the ordinate, and the ratio of the German money (M3) stock per unit of output divided by the US money stock M2 per unit of output, denoted MYGUS, is plotted on the abscissa.

[SF3]   The theory of uncovered interest rate parity with rational expectations claims that the expectation of the appreciation of the German mark from one period to the next is equal to the appropriate forward premium, equal to the appropriate foreign less German interest rate differential, at the initial period. This hypothesis is inconsistent with the evidence for Germany, as well as for other countries[8].

[SF4]   The real exchange rate is not cointegrated with the German terms of trade. This means that they are not the same variable[9].

---

[7] The German nominal price of the dollar DM/$ = DMUS = GRae, is plotted on the ordinate in figure 2. The money per unit of output in Germany is (M3/y) = (GR38nbc/GR99ar) and in the US it is (M2/y)' = (US59mbc/US99br). Hence the variable on the abscissa in figure 2 is the German to the US money per unit of output MYGUS = (GR38nbc/GR99ar)/(US59mbc/US99br). The sample period is 1973.1–1994.2. In this context, a rise in DM/$ implies a depreciation of the nominal DM. The ADF(C,0) = −1.88 is not significant even at the 10% level.

[8] This is a well known result. See, for example, Stein (1990, table 1), Stein (1994, figure 2).

[9] The ADF is not significant at the 10% level. The real effective exchange rate $R = Nw/w'$, the ratio of unit labor costs in the tradable sectors at home relative to abroad. The terms of trade $T = Np_x/q_m$, where p_x is the price of the German export good, q_m is the foreign price of imports and N is foreign currency/domestic currency. In a world of complete specialization R is proportional to T. This is seen as follows. Let (w, w') be domestic or foreign unit labor cost. Then $w = ap_x$ and $w' = bq_m$, where a and b represent labor's shares. Then $R = Nw/w' = N\, ap_x/bq_m = (Np_x/q_m)(a/b) = T(a/b)$. The real effective exchange rate is proportional to the terms of trade in a world of full specialization.

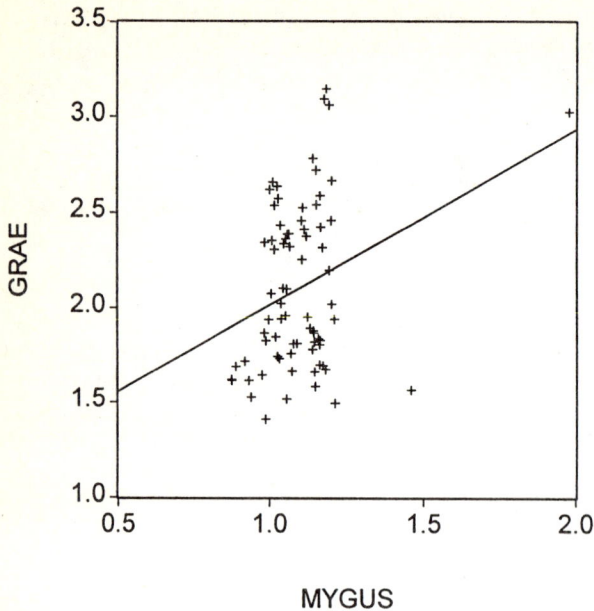

Fig. 2. DM per $US (DMUS) on vertical axis, ratio of German M3 to output, divided by US M2 to output (MYGUS) on horizontal axis.

[SF5] Since 1980, the German real long term rate of interest (GRINT) has converged to the US real long term rate of interest (USRINT). These variables are plotted in figure 3. We measure the real long term rate of interest by the nominal yield on bonds less the rate of inflation of the CPI over the past four quarters. The real long term rate of interest differential (GRINT-USRINT) is stationary at an expected value of zero[10] during the period 1980.1-1992.3. The German real long term rate of interest is Granger caused by the US rate, and not the reverse.

[SF6] The short term capital flows involving banks are stationary, with an expected value of zero[11]. This means that short term capital flows revert to a mean of zero.

[SF7] The ratio of the current account/GNP from 1973.1–1989.4 is not stationary. The ratio of German net foreign assets to GNP is not stationary. German net foreign assets are external assets less external liabilities. Germany started as a debtor in 1950, with net foreign assets/GNP of − 4%, and rose to a large creditor in 1989 with net foreign assets/GNP of 20%, before unification[12].

---

[10] The ADF(N, 1) = − 2.28 (MacKinnon 10% = − 1.6). No constant (N) was used because the constant was not significant.

[11] The ADF(N, 0) = − 8.0 which is significant at the 1% value.

[12] The data are from Masson, Kremers and Horne (table 6, 1993).

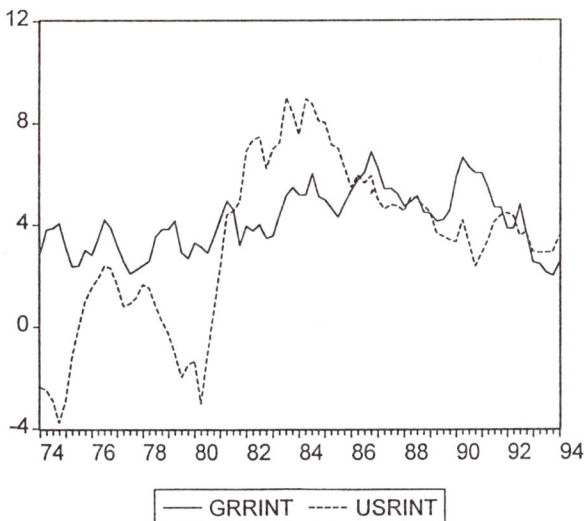

Fig. 3. German real long term rate of interest (GRINT), US real long term rate of interest (USRINT).

The Implications of the Stylized Facts

During the floating rate period [SF1] rejects PPP, which claims that the real exchange rate converges to a constant mean. The models of monetary dynamics with rational expectations, such as Dornbusch's 1976 model, imply that the strength of the DM is primarily due to the rationally expected German anti-inflationary monetary policies. This view would imply that the nominal DM/$US should be positively related to the ratio of money/real GNP in Germany compared to that in the US over the floating rate period. Figure 2 and [SF2] reject this hypothesis. Stylized facts 1, 2 and 3 reject the basic assumptions of the models of monetary dynamics with rational expectations, and the overshooting hypothesis.

The German terms of trade will be shown below to vary inversely with the prices of primary materials, which are exogenous. The real exchange rate however is an endogenous variable. That is an explanation of [SF4].

The implications of [SF5] are that Germany is small in the international financial markets and that there is no risk premium between the US and German real long term rates of interest.

The monetary dynamics-rational expectations models have been supplanted in the theoretical literature by the representative agent intertemporal optimization models (RAIOM). In these newer models there is a representative agent who makes a simultaneous saving-investment decision to optimize utility over an infinite horizon, subject to a constraint that the sum of the present value of absorption equal the sum of the present value of production plus the initial value of net foreign assets. Rogoff (1992) has made one of the few attempts to see if these models have explanatory power. These newer models make very restrictive and arbitrary assumptions[13]. Moreover, they do not lend themselves to empirical testing, because their crucial variables are anticipated or unanticipated productivity shocks, which cannot be measured in an objective way. The few attempts to apply the RAIOM to explain the data have been unsuccessful.

The theoretical contribution of the RAIOM models is that they are "forward looking", but the empirical measures of anticipations are just backward looking moving average processes, which are just adaptive expectations[14]. In Rogoff's study, the crucial variables which are proxies for anticipated or unanticipated productivity shocks turn out to be statistically insignificant and the one objective variable, government consumption spending, has the wrong sign.

Obsfeld and Rogoff (section 4.2.2) are cognizant of the failures of these models. They wrote: " ... it is unclear whether the intertemporal approach is simply false, or whether the many extraneous simplifications and maintained hypotheses imposed by the econometricians are to blame."

It is not appropriate to attribute the failure of these models to explain the empirical reality to the econometricians. On a very general level the implications of the RAIOM produce incredible results. Using "reasonable" estimates of parameters, Obstfeld and Rogoff (section 3.1.1) find that the theory implies that the steady state ratio of debt/GNP for a small open economy is 2000 per cent. This incredible result has nothing to do with the econometricians.

Stylized fact [SF7] rejects the main implication of the "Representative Agent Intertemporal Optimization Model" (RAIOM) for Germany. This model claims that the current account depends upon the deviations of interest rates, output, government spending and investment from their respective "permanent" levels[15]. Since these deviations are supposedly stationary with an expectation of zero, the current account should be stationary. This view is rejected by [SF7].

---

[13] Rogoff makes the following assumptions. (i) There is no intersectoral mobility of labor (p. 4). (ii) The present value of the excess demand for traded goods over an infinite horizon must equal the initial value of the representative agent's holding of net foreign assets (p. 5). (iii) There is no capital formation. (iv) The terms of trade are constant (p. 5). (v) The real rate of interest is constant (p. 10).

[14] Rogoff (1992, 24–25) states: "To separate out the anticipated components of productivity shocks, I use the autoregressions reported in table 4 ... a simple (1, 1, 0) process fits the data fairly well. The residuals from these regressions were used to proxy for unanticipated changes in lifetime traded goods income".

[15] Obstfeld and Rogoff (1995), equation (46). The general rejection of the RAIOM current account equation can be seen in their section 4.2.

The Logic of the Natural Real Exchange Rate (NATREX) Model: Summary and Conclusions

The NATREX model is a positive theory of what determines the basic trends of the real exchange rate. The real fundamentals are productivity and thrift, which is the complement of time preference. The NATREX is a general model which does not make the restrictive and arbitrary assumptions of the RAIOM. In this part we present the intuition behind the model and answer the questions posed at the beginning of this paper. In the subsequent parts, we present the formal model and empirical analyses.

Medium Run Effects

The NATREX is an equilibrium real exchange rate, when output is at capacity and the nonsustainable transitory speculative capital flows and changes in reserves are ignored. The NATREX equilibrates the current account to saving less investment, evaluated at capacity output[16].

A rise in the productivity of capital, measured by a rise in the Keynes-Tobin q-ratio, or a rise in time preference, measured by a rise in the ratio of social consumption/GNP, leads to a rise in investment less saving. The excess of investment over saving means that some of the investment is financed abroad, which generates a nonspeculative capital inflow. The real exchange rate appreciates and produces a current account deficit which finances the nonspeculative capital inflow[17].

Changes in time preference primarily occur because of changes in government policy. Time preference rose during the Schmidt period, fell during the Kohl period and rose as a result of the Government policies undertaken as a consequence of the German unification.

The Keynes-Tobin q-ratio is determined to a large extent by the European terms of trade, which is exogenous to Germany, and to the rate of capacity utilization which contains demand as well as supply effects.

---

[16] The equilibrium rate of exchange is evaluated at capacity output, but we do not discuss the mechanism of how capacity output is achieved. The same is true for the RAIOM. Hence the NATREX model differs from the Mundell-Fleming model which is an open economy Keynesian model. Our concept of an equilibrium exchange rate is quite similar to Nurkse's.

[17] The capital inflow which finances investment less saving may appreciate the nominal exchange rate. Alternatively, if the rise in excess demand is mainly for domestic goods, there will be a rise in the ratio of domestic to foreign trade weighted unit labor costs measured in a common currency (equation 1). It makes no difference in the model whether the real exchange rate appreciates because the nominal exchange rate appreciates or if the appreciation occurs because domestic nominal unit labor costs rise relative to the foreign nominal unit labor costs.

Longer Run Effects

Whereas higher capital productivity and higher time preference have the same effects upon the real exchange rate in the medium run, the longer run effects are different. In the longer run, the NATREX approach includes two stock adjustment processes. These stock adjustments come about because when there is balance of payments equilibrium in the medium run, there may be net investment and current account deficits or surpluses. The net investment changes the capital stock, and the current account changes the foreign debt. Either one of these changes wealth. There is then a feedback from the changes in the capital stock, foreign debt and wealth to investment, saving and the current account. The changes in debt and capital will then change the real exchange rate which equilibrates the balance of payments. In a dynamically stable system, the capital and debt intensities[18] converge to steady state levels. In the process, the real exchange rate converges to a steady state level.

The trajectories to the steady state as well as the steady state will depend upon whether the initial disturbance was to the productivity of capital or the time preference ratio. If the disturbance increased time preference because social consumption expenditures increased relative to GDP, the initial appreciation will change to a depreciation. The reason is that the current account deficits increase the foreign debt, which results in higher interest payments to foreigners. This tends to decrease the current account. A country could change from a creditor to a debtor, as a result of a rise in its time preference. Since the debt stabilizes in a dynamically stable system, the real exchange rate will depreciate to produce a trade surplus which will finance the interest payments to foreigners. The new long run real exchange rate is below its initial value. The cointegration equations show that a rise in time preference depreciates the longer run real value of the German mark.

A different trajectory occurs when the initial disturbance raises the q-ratio and hence the rate of investment. As the capital stock converges to its new steady state value, saving rises relative to investment and there will tend to be current account surpluses. The foreign debt will decline below its initial level, and the country can convert from a debtor to a creditor. The rise in interest income from abroad, or the decline in interest payments to foreigners, tends to appreciate the exchange rate. However, the rise in wealth tends to raise the value of imports relative to exports and tends to reduce the trade balance. The development of the real exchange rate is theoretically ambiguous in that case. However, the cointegrating equations show that a rise in the q-ratio appreciates the long run real exchange rate.

Our conclusion is that the trends in the real effective exchange rate are determined by the NATREX, which depends in a dynamic way upon productivity of capital and time preference, the inverse of thrift.

---

[18] The capital (debt) intensity is capital (debt) per effective worker. In the discussion we abstract from changes in effective labor.

The NATREX Model[19]

Our optimization and structural equations are general. They reflect optimization with feedback controls guaranteed to produce stability since there is uncertainty concerning the evolution of the exogenous variables. Equations (2)–(8) describe the NATREX model. There are seven basic endogenous variables and seven basic equations. The endogenous variables are: the real exchange rate[20] (NATREX), the real long term interest rate, the capital intensity, the debt intensity, consumption, saving and the q-ratio. The current account is the negative of the rate of change of foreign debt, or saving less investment.

Balance of Payments Equilibrium when there is Internal Balance

Equation (2) and the flow chart describe the role of the real exchange rate. Saving less investment $(S - I)$, discussed below, depend upon endogenous capital $k(t)$ and debt $F(t)$ and exogenous fundamentals $Z(t)$, which are time preference and the terms of trade which is an important determinant of the q-ratio. The real exchange rate $R(t)$ adjusts the current account CA to equal saving less investment generated by the fundamentals, when output is at capacity output, denoted $y(t) = y(k(t); Z(t))$, where $k(t)$ is the capital intensity and a parameter of productivity is an element in exogenous vector of fundamentals $Z(t)$. *The current account*[21] *ex post will be as "forward looking" as are the saving and investment functions, which are discussed below.* The line of causation in the flow chart runs from right to left. The LTK is the nonspeculative capital inflow, equal to investment less saving generated by the fundamentals.

$$CA(R, k, F; Z) <= LTK <= (I - S)(k, F; Z) <= Z$$

The current account $CA = B - rF$ is the trade balance B less interest payments to foreigners rF, where r is the real long term interest rate and F is the foreign debt $(+)$ or net foreign assets $(-)$. The trade balance is exports less imports, which depend upon the real exchange rate, foreign fundamentals (which determine exports and the terms of trade) domestic wealth equal to capital less debt, and domestic fundamentals (which determine imports). When the real exchange rate adjusts to

---

[19] The NATREX model is developed in Stein, Allen et al. (1995). It has been applied to the $US by Stein (1994) (1995). The chapter by Allen in Stein, Allen et al. places the model in perspective with the literature and evaluates its strengths and weaknesses.

[20] The actual real exchange rate is the real effective exchange rate GRREU. The theoretical equilibrium exchange rate, the NATREX, is denoted R.

[21] The inadequacy of the RAIOM models of the current account was discussed above, which explains why we do not take that approach.

produce balance of payments equilibrium, in the sense of equation (2) the current account will not necessarily be equal to zero.

$$CA(R(t, k(t), F(t); Z(t)) + (I - S)(k(t), F(t), r(t); Z(t)) = 0 \qquad (2)$$

We consider equation (2) as describing balance of payments equilibrium, for the following reason. Desired investment less saving $I - S$, equal to absorption less capacity output $y(k; Z)$, is the excess flow supply of long term securities plus short term securities plus domestic money. Our medium run equilibrium conditions assume that the short term capital flows and the excess supply of money average out to zero. We know from [SF6] that the short term capital flows reflected on bank balance sheets are stationary with an expected value of zero. We exclude them from an equilibrium concept of the real exchange rate, because they are not sustainable. Under these conditions $(I - S)$ corresponds to the nonspeculative long term capital inflow, denoted LTK. Equation (2) can then be viewed as stating that the real exchange rae adjusts the current account CA plus the nonspeculative capital inflow $LTK = (I - S)$, generated by the endogenous capital and debt and the exogenous fundamentals, to zero.

Portfolio Balance

Equation (3) states that German and US long term assets are close substitutes and there is no risk premium. Investors have long horizons and contemplate both direct and portfolio investment. The dominant long term rate of interest in the G7 is the US rate, denoted r'. The expected real return on German domestic long term assets is the real long term rate of interest r plus the expected long term appreciation of the DM which is the average annual appreciation denoted $E(DR)$ over a long horizon. The investors use all available information to form an expectation of the real appreciation or depreciation of the DM. Using all available information, the investors know (see the appendix) that the real effective German exchange rate $R(t)$ is integrated of order 1 and that the first differences are stationary with a zero expectation $E(DR) = 0$. Therefore, the rational expectation is that $E(DR) = 0$ over the investment horizon. In making their long term portfolio decision, investors just contemplate the real long term interest rate differential $(r - r')$.

This view is consistent with figure 3 which compares the German $(r = GRRINT)$ and US real long term interest rates $(r' = USRINT)$. Stylized fact [SF5] states that the differential $(r - r') = (GRRINT–USRINT)$ is stationary and has an expected value of zero[22]. When the German rate is below the US rate, there is a portfolio allocation away from German to US assets. The German real long term interest rate rises and the US rate declines. An analogous situation occurs when the

----

[22] The nominal or real short, or nominal long term nominal rates, do not converge.

German rate exceeds the US rate. The portfolio balance equation (3) is that German real long term rates have converged to the US level.

$$r(t) = r'(t) \tag{3}$$

Forward Looking Behavior with Feedback Control: Consumption, Saving and Investment

The failure of the RAIOM stems from the restrictive assumption that the entire economy can be modeled by a representative agent who chooses a time profile of consumption, subject to the constraint that the present value of the consumption stream equals the present value of the income stream plus initial net foreign assets. The RAIOM fails to specify any feedback control mechanism telling us how this constraint is to be achieved. Our generalization contains three parts. First, we have independent investment and saving functions. Second, there is a built in feedback control in the saving function designed to guarantee that the steady state debt converges to a constant. When that occurs, the current account is zero[23]. Third, there is a feedback control in the investment function designed to lead the economy to the unknown optimal trajectory.

Consumption and Saving Functions

Our intertemporal budget constraint is that the foreign debt stabilize, and not explode. We do this by introducing a feedback control into the optimal consumption equation. Formally, from the standard optimizing theory, social consumption C is proportional to permanent income Y^*. The latter is based upon the expectation that current income will grow at rate g and it is discounted at the real rate of interest r. This implies that social consumption, C is proportional to Y current income[24], denoted $C = cY$. The crucial exogenous parameter of the social consumption function is an index of time preference c equal to the ratio of private plus government consumption/GNP. Parameter c is an element of Z. A rise in the government budget deficit, not offset by a decrease in private consumption, is a rise in c. Transfer payments towards groups whose consumption to income ratio is high will also raise the index of time preference.

---

[23] For simplicity of exposition only, we assume that effective labor is constant.

[24] The derivation is as follows, where g is the expected growth rate and $r > g$ is the real rate of interest. $C(t) = c^* Y^* = c^* \int Y(t) e^{-(r-g)v} dv = c Y(t)$, where $t < v < \infty$. Parameter $c = \int c^* e^{-(r-g)v} dv = c^*/(r-g) > 0$ is our measure of time preference, and c^* is derived from the underlying utility functions.

We introduce a feedback control to guarantee that the debt stabilize. The public and private sectors form optimum profiles of intertemporal consumption, based upon their expectations of the present value of future income. The future evolution of income is unknown, and can only be guessed. The debt is then optimum consumption, based upon the initial expectations of the income profile, less realized income. If the realized debt exceeds the implied optimal profile of the debt, based upon earlier estimates of the income profile, then the consumption is reduced or saving is increased. In particular, the government decides upon a pattern of government consumption. It may do this according to the public choice models of government. Some of the government debt is foreign held. The growth of the debt is the budget deficit including the interest on the debt in the previous period. When the foreign debt rises to a level that the government realizes is unsustainable, then it changes its fiscal policy to reduce the deficit or increase government saving. The feedback control parameter is c'. A general social consumption function is equation (4), which contains the optimizing and feedback control components for the public[25] and private sectors combined.

$$c = cY - c'F \tag{4}$$

Saving S is GNP less consumption. The GNP is GDP less interest payments to foreigners rF. Hence the saving function[26] is equation (5). The debt has two effects upon saving: destabilizing and stabilizing. A rise in the debt lowers GNP because it increases the debt payments. This effect would decrease saving. However, a rise in the debt lowers consumption via the feedback control and raises saving. For stability, such that the foreign debt stabilize and not explode, the magnitude of the feedback control c' must exceed the real rate of interest.

$$S = (1-c)y(k;Z) + (c'-r)F = S(k, F, r; Z), \qquad S_F > 0 \tag{5}$$

Social consumption is negatively related, and the social saving is positively related, to the foreign debt. A rise in capital increases wealth and permanent income, and we expect that a rise in capital will raise saving[27].

---

[25] This approach to the role of the debt in the consumption function was inspired by G. P. Galli's criticisms of the earlier version of our paper given at the CIDEI conference.

[26] Saving = GNP − C = $[y(k;Z) - rF] - C$, where C is given by (4).

[27] We must allow the terms of trade T to affect saving, if the model is to be able to explain the evidence that an improvement in the terms of trade raises the current account. The current account is equal to saving less investment. A rise in the terms of trade must raise saving less investment. We explain this as follows. Saving is GDP less consumption, assuming no transfer income. Let the main component of GDP be the export good, whose price is p_x, and the main component of consumption is the import good whose price is p_m. The saving equation is (i) $S = p_x y(k;Z) - p_m C(k, F;Z)$. Insofar as we measure the real variables in terms of the export good, the saving equation is (ii) $S/p_x = y(k;Z) - C(k, F;Z)/T$. Hence saving is positively related to the terms of trade.

The Rate of Capital Formation

Equation (6) is the independent investment equation. In the standard optimal growth models, the Maximum Principle is used to derive the optimal rate of investment. This is an open loop control where we must have perfect knowledge. We must know with certainty the production function and the steady state capital intensity, denoted k^*. Then the optimal growth path is a saddle point path. The slightest error in our knowledge, the slightest deviation from the path, will send the economy off on an errant trajectory; and the economy will never reach the steady state. The use of the Maximum Principle is not feasible in economics because we do not have perfect knowledge and the unknown steady state is changing with the production function. One cannot be forward looking without perfect knowledge; and if there is not perfect knowledge, the economy will travel along an errant trajectory and never reach the optimal steady state. For this reason, Infante and Stein (RES, 1973) developed a closed loop suboptimal feedback control (SOFC) based upon dynamic programming. Our SOFC is guaranteed to home in on the unknowable optimal steady state capital intensity, and will be extremely close to the unknown optimum path. Disturbances will occur all of the time to the production function, which will change the currently measurable marginal product of capital and the unknown steady state. Our rate of investment will be adjusted, and will converge to the unknowable optimal trajectory. We have synthesized the optimal control for the realistic situation that there is not perfect knowledge and that the basic parameters are changing in an unknowable way. All that we require are observable measurements of the marginal product of capital. This generalizes the concept of forward looking behavior.

When saving and investment decisions are made independently, and when the capital good is not the same as the output, then Stein (1994) (1995, ch. 2, 3) made two changes in the SOFC. The optimal rate of investment is a nonlinear function of the Keynes-Tobin q-ratio based upon current measurements of variables. The rate of investment dk/dt will be positively related to the q-ratio so defined. When $q > 1$ then the rate of change of the capital intensity will be positive and when $q < 1$, the rate of change of the capital intensity will be negative.

$$dk/dt = I(q) \quad I(1) = 0, \ I'(q) > 0 \tag{6}$$

The q-ratio based upon current measurements is equation (7) below. It is the ratio of the capital value of an asset relative to its supply price. The capital value is the present value of the sum of the rents per unit of capital. The rent is the value of the marginal product of capital, the product of the output price and the marginal physical product of capital.

The output per unit of effective labor is $y(k(t); u(t))$ where $k(t)$ is the capital intensity and $u(t)$ is a parameter of productivity. Let $u(t)$ be an element in the vector of the exogenous variables $Z(t)$. The marginal physical product of capital is

$y'(k(t); Z(t))$. The output is assumed to the primarily in the export good whose current price is p_x. The rent per unit of capital is $p_x y'(k(t); Z(t))$.

The capital good is a composite of the export good (x) and the import good (m). The price of the capital good is $p_k = p_x^a p_m^{1-a}$, where a and $1 - a$ represent the weights of the export and import good. The terms of trade are $T = p_x/p_m$, which is an element in the exogenous vector Z.

Therefore, the rent per unit of capital divided by the supply price is $Ty'(k; Z)$. The ratio of the capital value to the supply price is the expected sum of the present values of $Ty'(k; Z)$. The expectation E is taken over the probability space of T, k and r. Making the substitution for the price of the capital good, the relevant q-ratio is positively related to the terms of trade $T(t)$, the current marginal physical product of capital $y'(k(t); Z(t))$, and negatively to the current real rate of interest r, where index v goes from t to infinity. The terms of trade are integrated of order $I(1)$. This means that the expectation of the terms of trade in the future is equal to the current terms of trade. Similarly, the US real rate of interest is $I(1)$. We may therefore obtain the last equality equation (7). The European terms of trade and US real interest rate are exogenous variables. In the steady state, the capital intensity $k = k*$ such that $q = 1$ which implies that the rent per unit capital divided by the reproduction cost is equal to the real rate of interest $T^{1-a} y'(k*; u) = r$.

$$q = E \int (p_x/p_k) y'(k(t); Z(t)) e^{-rv} dv = E \int T(t)^{1-a} y'(k(t); Z(t)) e^{-rv} dv$$
$$= T(t)^{1-a} y'(k(t); Z(t))/r = q(T, k, r; Z) \tag{7}$$

The Rate of Change of the Foreign Debt

The rate of change of the foreign debt dF/dt is described in equation (8). It is the current account deficit equal to investment less social saving, using equation (2)(5) and (6).

$$dF(t)/dt = I(q) - S(k(t), F(t); Z(t)) = -CA(R, k, F; Z) \tag{8}$$

Our intertemporal budget constraint is that the value of the foreign debt converges to a dynamically stable steady state (denoted by an asterisk) value $F*$. Stability means that the debt does not explode. This requires that $dS/dF > 0$ a rise in debt raises saving. In the steady state, where the debt is constant, investment less saving equal to the current account deficit is equal to zero. Then, the trade balance $B*$ must equal the interest payments $rF*$ on the foreign debt. This is long run external equilibrium.

Solution of the Model[28]

The model is solved in two steps. The first step, which we call the medium run, takes the capital and debt as parameters. The system is solved for the real exchange rate and real long term rate of interest, which simultaneously produce balance of payments equilibrium equation (2), and portfolio balance equation (3). The second step concerns the evolution of the stocks of capital (equations (6)–(7)), and debt (equation (8)). The endogenous variations in capital and debt then feed back and affect the medium run solution for the real exchange rate in the first step.

Medium Run

Equation (2), using the equations (5)–(7) for saving and investment, can be viewed graphically in the space of real exchange rate and real long term interest rate. Each curve labelled IX in figure 4 is the set of real exchange rates and real long term rates of interest which satisfies equation (2), given the value of capital, debt and exogenous fundamentals[29]. Each IX curve is negatively sloped in the space of real exchange and real long term interest rates, because a rise in the real rate of interest raises saving less investment evaluated at capacity output. This increases the nonspeculative capital outflow. A depreciation of the real exchange rate will increase the competitiveness of the economy and increase the trade balance, to offset the capital outflow generated by the rise in the interest rate. All along each IX curve there is balance of payments equilibrium at capacity output.

The real exchange rate will be driven to the IX curve, associated with the given levels of capital, debt and fundamentals. When the economy is below the IX curve, the current account plus the nonspeculative capital inflow is positive; and there is an excess demand for the German currency relative to foreign currency. Since the long term nonspeculative capital inflow is investment less saving, there is an excess demand for German goods at capacity output. Then either the nominal DM will appreciate or domestic unit labor costs will rise relative to their foreign counterparts[30]. The appreciation of the real exchange rate will decrease the current account and the economy will converge to the IX curve.

The portfolio balance equation (3) is described by the PB curve in figure 4. Insofar as the German real long term rate of interest r deviates from the US rate r', there will be a shift between German mark and \$US denominated assets. This

---

[28] A mathematical solution and stability conditions are in the Stein (1994) and Stein, Allen et al. (1995) references. Hence a graphic and intuitive discussion here will suffice.

[29] The IX curve is the set of (R, r) such that $I - S + CA = 0$, given (k, F, Z) and that y is at capacity output. As $(k, F; Z)$ varies, the IX curve shifts.

[30] A similar argument applies when the economy is above the IX curve.

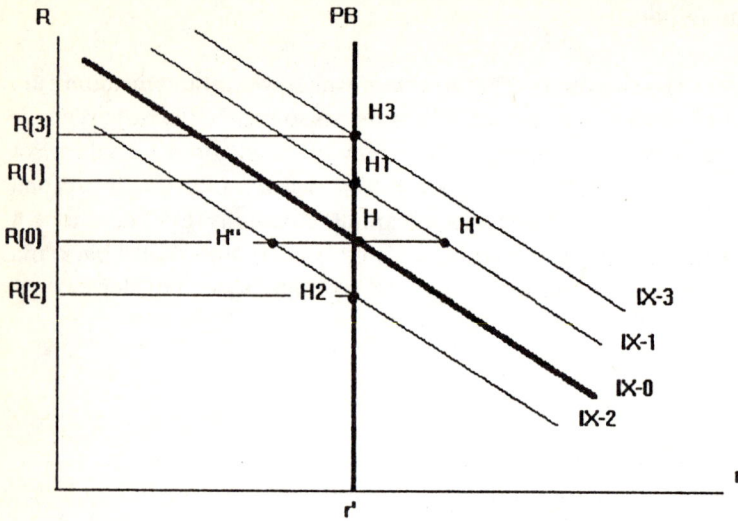

Fig. 4. Each IX curve represents balance of payments equilibrium equation (2), given capital, debt and fundamentals. The PB curve represents portfolio balance equation (3).

reallocation of portfolios will lead to a convergence of the real long term rates of interest to the PB curve.

The real exchange rate and real rate of interest which simultaneously produce balance of payments equilibrium and portfolio balance is equation (9), described by the intersection of the IX and PB curves.

$$R(t) = R[k(t), F(t); Z(t)] \quad Z = \{c, T, r', u\} \tag{9}$$

This is our NATREX, for given values of capital, debt and fundamentals. Cyclical and transitory factors, such as short term capital movements are not considered in the set of fundamentals. They affect the deviations of the real effective exchange rate from the NATREX in equation (9). This is the first stage of the solution.

The Evolution of Capital and Debt

The IX curves associated with balance of payments equilibrium will shift with endogenous variations in capital, debt and the exogenous fundamentals. This evolution is stage two of the solution. The evolution of capital is given by equation (10) which is based upon equations (6) (7) and (3).

$$dk(t)/dt = J(k(t); Z(t)) \tag{10}$$

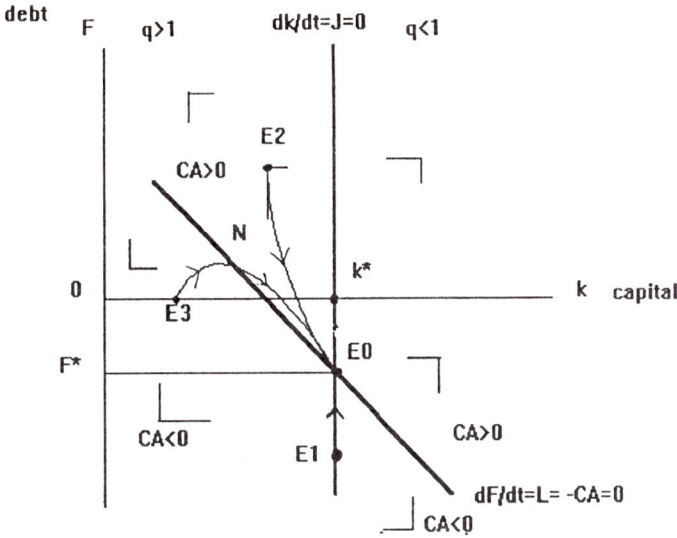

Fig. 5. Phase diagram for the evolution of capital and debt. Along the $J=0$ curve, the q-ratio is unity. Along the $L=0$ curve the current account is zero.

The vertical curve $J=0$ in figure 5 describes the equation $dk/dt = J(k; Z) = 0$. The horizontal vectors indicate the directions of movement of capital. At a capital intensity of k^*, the q-ratio will be unity and the capital intensity will not be changing. At that point the rent per unit of capital/supply price is equal to the real US rate of interest[31]. When the capital intensity is less than k^*, the q-ratio exceeds unity because the decline in the capital intensity raises the marginal product of capital.

Equation (11), based upon (8) and (10), describes the evolution of the foreign debt. The negatively sloped curve $dF/dt = (J-S) = L = 0$ in figure 5 is the relation between debt and capital such that investment less saving is zero $(J-S) = L = 0$.

$$dF(t)/dt = J(k(t); Z(t)) - S(k(t), F(t); Z(t)) = L(k(t), F(t); Z(t)) \qquad (11)$$

Since we have goods market clearing along the IX curve, function $(J-S)$ is equal to the current account deficit. Along the $L=0$ curve, the current account is zero, and the foreign debt is not changing. It is negatively sloped for the following reason. A rise in capital raises saving less investment, which produces a capital outflow and reduces the debt. Hence the slope is negative. Given capital, the debt converges to the $L=0$ curve in our stable system, which satisfies our intertemporal budget constraint. A rise in the foreign debt above the $L=0$ curve raises saving. The rise in

---

[31] The condition that $q=1$ is $T^{1-a}y'(k^*; u) = r$.

saving less investment produces a capital outflow which reduces the foreign debt back to the $L = 0$ curve. The element of stability $L_F = \delta(dF/dt)/\delta F < 0$ produces our intertemporal budget constraint, whereby the debt stabilizes at value $F^*(Z)$.

Summary of the Dynamics from the Medium to the Long Run

The NATREX at any time is equation (9), a function of capital, debt and the fundamentals $Z(t)$. Capital evolves according to equation (10), and debt evolves according to equation (11). Therefore, the real exchange rate evolves according to equation (12), based upon (9)–(11).

$$dR(t)/dt = R_k J(k(t); Z(t)) + R_F L(k(t), F(t); Z(t)) \tag{12}$$

Capital will converge to k^* where the q-ratio is unity, along the $J(k; Z) = 0$ curve in figure 5. Debt will converge to $F^*(Z(t))$ where the current account is zero, along the $L(k, F; Z) = 0$ curve in figure 5. In the steady state the trade balance B^* must be sufficient to pay the interet on the foreign debt $r'F^*(Z)$. Equations $J = 0$ and $L = 0$ determine the steady state values of capital and debt as functions of the fundamentals, denoted $k^* = k^*(Z(t))$ and $F^* = F^*(Z(t))$. We denote the steady state of a variable with an asterisk[32].

The steady state real exchange rate, denoted $R^*(Z(t))$ in equation (13), produces balance of payments equilibrium when there is portfolio equilibrium (figure 4), and when capital and debt are at their steady state values.

$$R^*(t) = R[k^*(Z(t), F^*(Z(t)); Z(t)] = R^*[Z(t)]. \tag{13}$$

Variable $R^*(Z(t))$ is a moving long run equilibrium, which moves with the fundamentals. The PPP theory which claims that the long run real exchange rate is stationary will be valid if and only if a linear combination of the fundamentals is stationary. The condition that the right hand side of (13) is stationary will not necessarily occur over the period considered.

Data and the German Historical Experience

We use quarterly data that correspond as closely as possible to the variables in the theoretical analysis. The source, measurement and history of the evolution of the exogenous variables in vector Z is the subject of this section. All of the series we use are plotted in figure 6, over the sample period 1975:2–1993:3.

---

[32] The steady state is described by these equations. $J(k^*; Z) = 0$, $L(k^*, F^*; Z) = 0$, $R^* = R(k^*, F^*; Z)$, where the asterisk denotes the steady state. The detailed mathematics are in the Stein references above concerning the NATREX model.

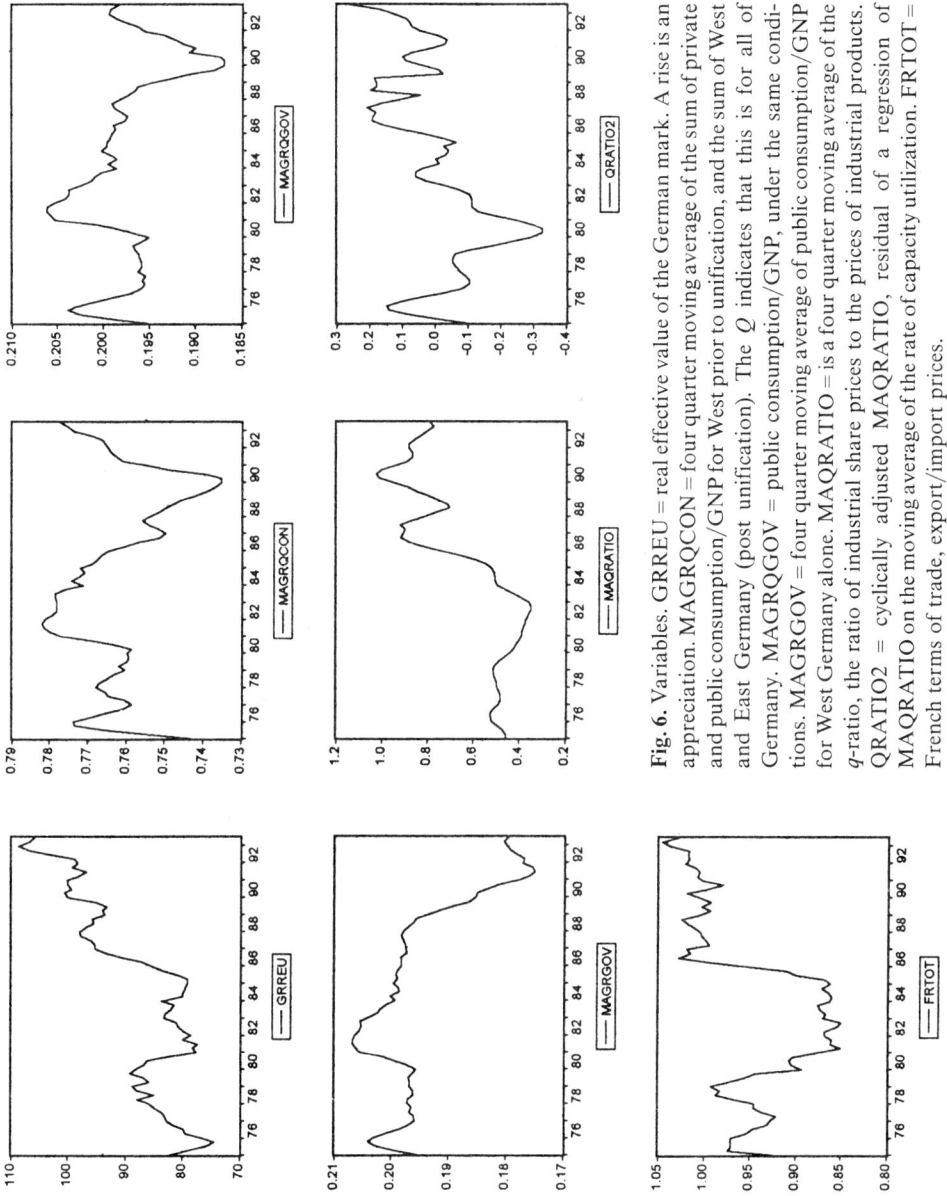

Fig. 6. Variables. GRREU = real effective value of the German mark. A rise is an appreciation. MAGRQCON = four quarter moving average of the sum of private and public consumption/GNP for West prior to unification, and the sum of West and East Germany (post unification). The Q indicates that this is for all of Germany. MAGRQGOV = public consumption/GNP, under the same conditions. MAGRGOV = four quarter moving average of public consumption/GNP for West Germany alone. MAQRATIO = is a four quarter moving average of the q-ratio, the ratio of industrial share prices to the prices of industrial products. QRATIO2 = cyclically adjusted MAQRATIO, residual of a regression of MAQRATIO on the moving average of the rate of capacity utilization. FRTOT = French terms of trade, export/import prices.

The real exchange rate in the model is the relative price that equates the current account to saving less investment generated by the fundamentals. We have elected to use the real effective exchange rate (GRREU) in equation (1) because it is the ratio of German prices of tradables relative to trade weighted prices of tradable of her competitors. This variable is not stationary, the ADF = − 0.848.

The exogenous variables are time preference for consumption, coefficient c in equation (4), and the productivity of capital measured by the Keynes-Tobin q-ratio.

1. Time Preference

We used several different measures of time preference. Time preference in the model is social time preference, which is public plus private consumption to GNP. The social consumption/GNP and the government consumption/GNP move together.

First we used IMF International Financial Statistics data for government consumption/GNP, denoted GRGOV. The national income accounts in the IFS *refer only to West Germany.* Since most series are seasonal, we take four quarter moving averages, denoted by a prefix MA. One measure of time preference is MAGRGOV. This variable is not stationary. The ADF = − 1.11.

Second, we used data which cover both West Germany prior to the unification and to all of Germany after unification[33]. For time preference we used the sum of West and East German government nominal consumption divided by the sum of West and East German nominal GNP. The derived series is called GRQGOV, where *the Q refers to all of Germany post unification.* The four quarter moving average, to correct for seasonality, is MAGRQGOV. This is stationary with an ADF = − 3.12.

Third, we also used a four quarter moving average of social consumption/ GNP for *all of Germany,* post unification. It is a moving average of the sum of West and East German private plus government consumption divided by the sum of West and East German GNP. The series, referred to as MAGRQCON, is stationary with an ADF = − 2.99.

The two series for all of Germany post unification, government time preference MAGRQGOV and social time preference MAGRQCON, move together[34]. However, there is a big difference between the series from the IFS based

---

[33] The source of the underlying data is Volkswirtschaftliche Gesamtrechnungen des Statistischen Bundesamtes, Fachserie 18, Sonderdruck 8; –, Fachserie 18, Reihe 3, Ausgabe 1/87, 1/89, 1/91, 2/92; –, Vierteljahresergebnisse der Inlandsproduktberechnung, Marz 1995. We thank Robert Grassinger for supplying us with these data.

[34] This fact is inconsistent with Ricardian Equivalence. Compare social time preference MAGRQCON with government time preference is MAGRQGOV in figure 6. These variables refer to unified Germany.

upon West German data, MAGRGOV and the series MAGRQGOV, MAGRQ-CON based upon data from both West and East Germany post unification. The data from West Germany alone[35] (i) are not stationary, and (ii) do not pick up the significant rise in social consumption after the unification. The series for all of Germany MAGRQGOV, MAGRQCON (i) are stationary and (ii) show the rise in time preference clearly. We just consider the data for unified Germany.

The history of the time preference variables reflects the German political situation. From 1969–82 the Social Democratic party was in power, led from 1974 by Schmidt. After a period of expansionary fiscal policies in the first half of the seventies, the Schmidt government, during the period 1977–79, tried to stabilize the share of government consumption/GDP. Government debt which grew rapidly in the mid seventies could not be reduced by that strategy, but its growth could be slowed down. At the Bonn summit in mid 1978, however, Schmidt agreed that Germany should be a locomotive for growth. He put in force government expenditure programs, and government consumption/GNP began to rise again in 1980–82 period. The time preference graphs of MAGRQGOV, MAGRQCON in figure 6 show this clearly.

Social time preference MAGRQCON shows a rapid rise until 1982 for an additional reason. After his election, the Brandt government promised not to accept any unemployment. This promise made it impossible for trade union leaders to oppose the wage demands from the rank and file. As a result, there were large wage increases in 1973–75, especially in the public sector[36], which raised social time preference.

From 1982–90 government time preference MAGRQGOV declined drastically. This decline coincided with the switch from a Social Democratic government to a Conservative government led by Kohl. It was part of Kohl's government program to slow down public deficits[37]. This reduced government time preference MAGRQGOV. In addition, wage pressures remained weak possibly as a result of the severe 1981–82 depression and the substitution of Kohl for Schmidt. During the Kohl period prior to unification 1982–90, we see a decline in both measures of time preference, government MAGRQGOV and social MAGRQCON[38].

---

[35] This is true for either measure of time preference based upon the IFS data, which just refer to West Germany.

[36] In 1974, one year after the oil price increase, wage increases of 12% were negotiated.

[37] This is consistent with the feedback control parameter c' in our equation (4) for the consumption function. We are indebted to G. P. Galli for this idea, in his criticism of an earlier draft of this paper at the CIDEI conference in Rome.

[38] We shall discuss the post unification period later.

2. The Expected Return on Investment, the q-ratio

The second fundamental exogenous variable is the Keynes-Tobin q-ratio which affects the investment function. It is the ratio of the capital value of an asset relative to its reproduction cost. We calculate it as the ratio of industrial share prices to the prices of industrial products, QRATIO = GR62/GR63 in the IFS. This variable is seasonal, so we used a four quarter moving average denoted MAQRATIO, graphed in figure 6. This variable is not stationary: the ADF = −1.14.

Equation (7) shows that the q-ratio depends upon the terms of trade, the marginal physical product of capital and the real long term rate of interest. Two measurable determinants of the MAQRATIO are the terms of trade and the capacity utilization rate. The German terms of trade is fundamental exogenous variable in our model. Arithmetically, it is contained in the real exchange rate[39]. Therefore we used the European terms of trade as our exogenous variable, and took the French terms of trade denoted FRTOT, defined as FR74/FR75 from the IFS, as our measure of the European terms of trade.

Since the q-ratio is cyclical, we also calculated a cyclically adjusted measure by regressing MAQRATIO upon a four quarter moving average of the capacity utilization rate in manufacturing. The residual, denoted QRATIO2, is a cyclically and seasonally adjusted measure of the Keynes-Tobin q-ratio.

Compare[40] the cyclically adjusted QRATIO2 with the French terms of trade FRTOT plotted in figure 6. There are two main movements in the French terms of trade series. The price of imported materials is the factor producing the large swings in the terms of trade. The French terms of trade index declined from 1978–80 as a result of the second oil shock. The QRATIO2 declined during that period. The FRTOT rose from 1984 to 1986 as prices of imported materials declined. This decline occurred because the dollar prices of these materials declined, and the value of the dollar also declined relative to the mark[41]. The QRATIO2 rose significantly during this period. A regression from 1975:1–1993:3 of the MAQRATIO upon the French terms of trade and the capacity utilization rate yields positive and very significant coefficients and an R-squared of 0.8. Thus, during the period prior to the German unification, the q-ratio was determined by the European terms of trade and the capacity utilization rate. The prices of imported materials dominated the movements in the European terms of trade.

---

[39] See note 9 above.

[40] The comparison is even clearer if we normalize the variables QRATIO2 and FRTOT and put them on the same graph. To save space, we just display figure 6.

[41] Looking at annual, rather than quarterly, data concerning the prices of imported materials in Germany, the index (1985 = 100) rises from 41 in 1978 to 97 in 1982. Then it declines from 99 in 1984 to 47 in 1988. See Sauernheimer and Grassinger.

Econometric Methodology and Results[42]

In this part we discuss the econometric methodology and summarize the results. The detailed econometrics are discussed in the appendix tables A1 and A2. Our main contribution is in the next part, where we show how the NATREX model explains the empirical phenomena.

The theory and econometrics can be related as follows. The evolution of the real exchange rate can be seen from identity (14), a sum of three terms.

$$GRREU(t) = [GRREU(t) - R(k(t), F(t); Z(t))] + [R(k(t), F(t); Z(t)) - R^*(Z(t))]$$
$$+ [R^*(Z(t))] \tag{14}$$

The first term concerns how the actual real exchange rate $GRREU(t)$ converges to the NATREX which is $R(k(t), F(t); Z(t))$ in equation (9). At any time, transitory speculative and cyclical elements produce deviations between the real effective exchange rate GRREU and the NATREX. The model claims that these deviations, the first term in (14), average out to zero. The second term involves the evolution of NATREX as capital and foreign debt evolve over time, based upon equations (10) (11) and phase diagram figure 5. The last term is the steady state NATREX equation (13) when capital and debt, associated with the given value of $Z(t)$, are no longer changing.

Econometric Methodology

The econometrics of cointegration attempt to disentangle the longer run equilibrium of a relationship from the movements towards the equilibrium. Let R be the real exchange rate and Z a vector of exogenous variables of productivity and time preference. A dynamic process, equations (9)–(11), is specified by the model. The dynamic system to be estimated is equation (15). The steady state $R(t) = BZ(t)$, is associated with the cointegrating equation. The error correction term $b[R(t-1) - BZ(t-1)]$ relates to the dynamic adjustment term $[R(k(t), F(t); Z(t)) - R^*(Z(t))]$. The term $e(t)$ relates to deviation of the actual from the theoretical exchange rate $[GRREU(t) - R(k(t), F(t); Z(t))]$, which should have a zero expectation.

$$R(t) = \mathbf{B}Z(t) + b[R(t-1) - \mathbf{B}Z(t-1)] + e(t) \tag{15}$$

---

[42] The econometric cointegration methodology is discussed in the note by Lim (this issue). We attempt to take into account Clark's comments (this issue).

For reasons discussed in Lim's paper below, we use a nonlinear least squares estimation of vector B, which is constrained to be the same in the first and second terms of (15), written in bold letters. A main object in the econometrics is to estimate the longer run effects described by vector B in (15).

Econometric Results[43]

Our results concerning the cointegrating part $R = BZ$ in equation (15) can be summarized as follows. The variables graphed in figure 6 refer to unified Germany. (i) Either social MAGRQCON or government MAGRQGOV time preference depreciates the real exchange rate[44]. (ii) The q-ratio, MAQRATIO appreciates the longer run value of the German mark. (iii) The dummy variable, referring to pre and post unification, is significant. This indicates that the unification led to an appreciation over and above what was predicted from the measured values of the exogenous variables. (iv) The capacity utilization rate variable was not significant.

Figure 7 graphs the actual real effective exchange rate GRREU and the medium and long run values of the NATREX, based upon appendix table A2. We refer to $BZ(t)$ as the longer run NATREX, labelled NATREXG1 in figure 7. The medium run NATREX, labelled as GRREUF in figure 7, is the sum of the longer run value $BZ(t) =$ NATREXG1 and the error correction part $b[\text{GRREU}(t-1) - \text{NATREXG1}(t-1)]$. The relation among these variables in figure 7 is described by equations (16a)–(16b), based upon (14) (15).

$$\text{NATREXG1}(t) = BZ(t) \tag{16}$$

$$\text{GRREUF}(t) = \text{NATREXG1}(t)$$
$$+ b[\text{GRREU}(t-1) - \text{NATREXG1}(t-1)] \tag{16a}$$

$$\text{GRREU}(t) = \text{GRREUF}(t) + e(t) \tag{16b}$$

Figure 7 shows that the actual real effective exchange rate GRREU always converges to the GRREUF, which is the medium run NATREX. Until unification, the actual real effective exchange rate also converged to the longer run value NATREXG1. The deviations are stationary[45] with a zero expectation, and are not long lasting.

---

[43] The technical econometric analysis is described in the appendix.

[44] In appendix table A1, government time preference MAGRQGOV is used; and in appendix table A2 social time preference MAGRQCON is used. The results are almost identical.

[45] The ADF of the difference (GRREU–NATREXG1), during the period 1975:1–1990:3, is -3.27, which is stationary.

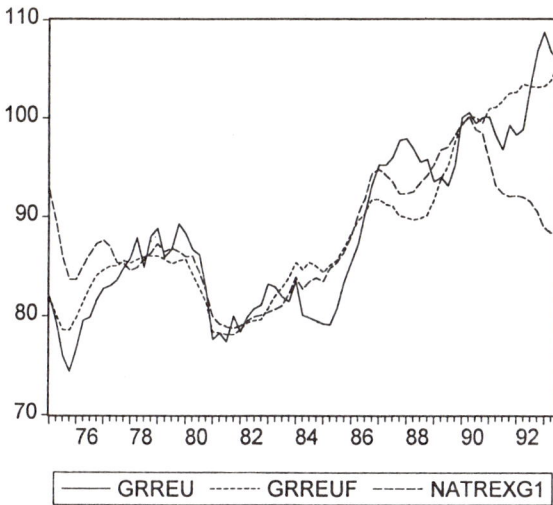

Fig. 7. The real effective exchange rate is GRREU. The medium run NATREX is GRREUF and the longer run value is NATREXG1.

After unification, the medium run GRREUF appreciated. The actual real effective exchange rate appreciated and converged to the GRREUF, the medium run NATREX. However, the longer run component NATREXG1 declined because of the rise in time preference. In the post unification period, although the actual real effective exchange rate was close to its *medium run* value, it was far above the long run equilibrium value. The errors between GRREU and the *long run* value NATREXG1 are large and are not stationary. We now use the NATREX model to explain these results.

Interpretation of the Results in terms of the NATREX Model

The NATREX explanation of the movements of the German real effective exchange rate, summarized at the beginning of the paper, is now done in terms of equation (9)–(11). These equations are described in figures 4 and 5. The variables are graphed in figure 6. The theoretical arguments of the effects of changes in the fundamentals Z upon the real effective exchange rate, discussed in this part, are summarized in table 1, rows a–b. Row a refers to the medium run, described in figure 4. Row b refers to the trajectory to the steady state point $E0$ in figure 5. Row c refers to the econometric results in appendix tables A1 and A2.

German Time Preference

Let the initial position be point H in figure 4 and point $E1$ in figure 5. The Schmidt policies increased time preference (MAGRQGOV or MAGRQCON) and lowered

Table 1. Summary of the effects of time preference and the q-ratio, either resulting from a rise in terms of trade or from a rise in the productivity of capital upon the NATREX in the medium and longer run

---

1. Rise in German time preference (MAGRQGOV) or (MAGRQCON)
   a. medium run, figure 4: $H - H' - H1$ appreciation $R(1) > R(0)$
   b. trajectory $E1$–$E0$ (figure 5), decrease in current account, rise in debt, longer run depreciation $R(2) < R(0)$
   c. cointegrating equation: rise in MAGRQGOV or MAGRQCON depreciates real value of DM

2. Rise in German q-ration (MAQRATIO) due to the European terms of trade
   a. medium run, figure 4: $H - H' - H1$ appreciation, $R(1) > R(0)$
   b. longer run trajectory (figure 5) $E2$–$E0$. Increase in current account and decrease debt. The decline in debt leads to an appreciation above $R(1)$. The increase in capital per se leads to a depreciation below $R(1)$. Net effect is ambiguous, but expect appreciation above $R(0)$
   c. cointegrating equation: rise in (MAQRATIO) appreciates real value of DM

3. Rise in German q-ratio (MAQRATIO) due to a rise in the productivity of capital
   a. medium run $H - H1$ appreciation
   b. longer run trajectory (figure 5):
      along segment $E3 - N$, there is a decrease in current account, rise in debt, depreciation; along segment $N - E0$: The increase in current account decreases debt and leads to an appreciation. The increase in capital leads to a depreciation. Net effect is theoretically ambiguous
   c. cointegrating equation: rise in (MAQRATIO) appreciates real value of DM

---

social saving. There was a rise in investment less social saving. The rise in time preference shifts the IX curve from IX–0 to IX–1 in figure 4. The decline in social saving raises aggregate demand and the real rate of interest rises to H', which exceeds the world rate r'. The excess of investment less saving is financed by a capital inflow. The capital inflow reduces the German real long term interest rate back to the world level r', and the real effective exchange rate appreciates from initial real exchange rate $R(0)$ to $R(1)$. The movement $H - H' - H1$ in figure 4 restores both the equality of the current account plus the nonspeculative capital inflow (at capacity output) to zero, and portfolio equilibrium.

At $H1$ the capital inflow is offset by a current account deficit. This means that the economy is at point $E1$ in figure 5. There are current account deficits, so the foreign debt rises (or foreign assets decline). The trajectory is $E1$–$E0$ to the steady state[46] with a higher debt F^*. The higher debt increases saving and decreases the current account, due to the rise in net interest payments. This factor shifts the IX curve downwards below IX–0 to IX–2. The initial appreciation of the real exchange rate to $R(1) > R(0)$ is more than offset. The real exchange rate along

---

[46] The q-ratio does not change because the real long term rate of interest remains at r', the world level. Hence the capital intensity k^* does not change.

trajectory $E1$–$E0$ ends up at $R(2)$ which is below $R(0)$. The Schmidt policy first appreciated the real exchange rate $R(1) > R(0)$, as it raised aggregate demand. It then led to a depreciation to $R(2)$ below its initial level $R(0)$, as a result of the lower net foreign assets or higher debt due to the decline in the current account. In the steady state, the current account is zero. The trade balance must equal the interest payments. Since the debt is higher, the interest payments are higher. The real exchange rate must depreciate to increase the trade balance to offset the flow of interest payments.

The decline in time preference under Kohl (MAGRQGOV or MAGRQCON) from 1982–93 produced effects which were the reverse of the Schmidt policies. Although the decline in time preference was to depreciate the real value of the currency in the *medium run,* an important factor explaining the *trend rise* in the NATREX during the Kohl period was the decline in social time preference.

The Rise in the q-Ratio Resulting
from a Rise in the European Terms of Trade

During the period prior to unification, the q-ratio was primarily determined by the European terms of trade. The terms of trade are primarily affected by rising or falling imports prices, which are exogenous to Germany. We now explain the terms of trade effect in terms of the NATREX model.

Start at point H in figure 4 and point $E2$ in figure 5. Consider a rise in the terms of trade (1985–87). Initially, the IX curve is IX-0, the portfolio balance curve is PB and the real exchange rate is at point $R(0)$. A rise in the terms of trade raises the current account directly and stimulates investment as a result of the rise in q-ratio. The IX curve shifts from IX-0 to IX-1. The real effective exchange rate appreciates to $R(1)$ to equilibrate the balance of payments. The appreciation of the real exchange rate partially offsets the effect of a rise in the terms of trade upon the current account, and the improvement in terms of trade raises saving. At point $H1$, both the current account and saving less investment have increased[47].

As a result of the rise in the terms of trade, the economy is at point $E2$ in phase diagram figure 5. There is a positive current account and the q-ratio has risen. Induced capital accumulation raises the capital intensity to k^*. The current account surpluses lead to a decline in the debt. The economy follows trajectory $E2$–$E0$ to the new steady state. The debt stabilizes at a lower level F^*. The decline in the debt decreases saving, increases the current account due to the decline in interest payments, and shifts the IX curve further above IX-1 to IX-3 in figure 4. The rise in capital partially offsets this rise. The final result is that the

---

[47] This is why it was necessary for us to explain, in connection with equation (5) footnote 27 above, why a rise in the terms of trade must increase saving.

real effective exchange rate appreciates above its initial level $R(0)$. This was the 1985–87 scenario. When the terms of trade declined (1979–81), the argument goes in reverse.

German Unification

The Basic Facts

The treaty of economic and currency unification 1 July 1990 integrated both parts of Germany. It was expected that the German unification would present a laboratory situation to study the consequences of a rise in the productivity of capital and a rise in time preference.

Prior to unification, the main movements in the q-ratio were due to movements in the terms of trade. After unification, figure 6 shows that, for all of Germany, the cyclically adjusted q-ratio QRATIO2 rose significantly[48] with no significant rise in terms of trade. There were three reasons for the rise in the q-ratio after unification. Since the capital intensity in East Germany was very low compared to West Germany, the German capital intensity in unified Germany declined substantially after unification. There was a technology transfer from West to East. The rebuilding of the East German infrastructure raises the productivity of private capital. These factors would raise the q-ratio significantly in the unified Germany.

Time preference rose for several reasons. The East Germans were endowed with German marks from the currency conversion, and would have access to western goods. The massive transfers from West to East, giving the East Germans access to Western goods, further increased the overall time preference measure. In East Germany after unification,[49] consumption plus investment exceeded GDP. Net imports to East Germany were 92% of her GDP in 1991, 82% in 1992 and 66% in 1993. A very large part of these imports were financed from West German transfer payments. These transfers consisted of payments from the federal government, the West German social security system, and a special "German Unity" fund. In 1993, the fiscal transfers to East Germany amounted to 6 per cent of West German GNP.

West German consumption did not decline to offset the higher East German consumption. The time preference for unified *West and East* Germany (MAGRQ-GOV and MAGRQCON) rose significantly after unification, as shown figure 6.

---

[48] The noncyclically adjusted MAQRATIO declined due to the recession. Compare the MAQRATIO with QRATIO2 in figure 6.

[49] We are drawing upon Clausen and Willms, especially their tables 1 and 2, for the description of East Germany. See Sinn and Sinn, Clausen and Willms, and Friedmann and Herrmann for the effects of unification.

The use of West German data MAGRGOV (without the Q) does not reflect the significant rise in time preference in unified Germany.

There was a large increase in investment in East Germany. In 1993, per capita investment was the same in both parts of Germany. Government investment in East Germany is mainly in infrastructure, carried out by the German Federal Post Office and Railway Company. Private investment is almost exclusively in capital intensive-labor saving activities. These private investments are subsidized by 20 to 30 per cent. The rise in domestic expenditure in East Germany has been a mixture of private and public increases in time preference. Part of the rise in investment is engendered by a rise in the q-ratio and part of it is a result of subsidies.

The Analysis [50]

The medium run effects of either the rise in time preference or the q-ratio increases investment less saving. These effects shift the IX curve from IX(0) to IX(1) in figure 4, and appreciate the real value of the German mark from $R(0)$ to $R(1)$. The rise in time preference leads to a long run depreciation, as described above. The rise in the q-ratio [51] leads to a long run appreciation. The longer run effects depend upon the magnitude of the rise in time preference relative to the rise in productivity of capital.

The expected scenario in the longer run, resulting from a rise in the q-ratio, corresponds to the stages of economic growth. The rise in the q-ratio places the economy at point $E3$ in figure 5. There is a rise in the capital intensity because the q-ratio rises. There is a capital inflow to finance the rise in investment relative to saving. There are current account deficits to finance investment less saving. The first part of the trajectory of the economy is $E3$–N, where the capital and debt intensities rise.

The rise in capital and debt along $E3$–N lower the current account due to the rise in imports and debt payments. Hence, when the economy travels along $E3$–N, the IX curve in figure 4 shifts down, thereby offsetting the initial appreciation.

Eventually as capital rises with the reconstruction of Eastern Germany, GDP will rise. Saving increases relative to investment along the second part of the trajectory N–$E0$. The current account deficits turns into current account surpluses, and the debt declines.

The rise in capital and decline in the debt have offsetting effects upon the IX curve. The decline in the debt raises the current account, shifts the IX curve upwards, and appreciates the real effective exchange rate. The rise in capital raises GDP, saving less investment and tends to shift the IX curve downwards. It is a

---

[50] Table 1 summarizes this analysis.

[51] The q-ratio rises because the marginal physical productivity of capital $y'(k; u)$ increases. The technology transfer and infrastructure raise parameter u, an element of Z.

force of depreciation. Theoretically the net effect is ambiguous. The equations in the appendix tables A1, A2 show that a rise in the q-ratio appreciates the real exchange rate.

Conclusion

The NATREX model defines the fundamental determinants of the equilibrium real effective exchange rate in the medium to longer run. The PPP theory is a special case of the NATREX when a linear combination of the fundamentals, which are productivity and social thrift, is stationary. The differences in social thrift under Schmidt and Kohl, and the effects of the European terms of trade upon the q-ratio, explain the variations in the NATREX in the preunification period. The actual real exchange rate of the German mark converged to both the medium run and longer run values of the NATREX.

In the postunification period, the medium run NATREX increased due to the rise in time preference and the cyclically adjusted q-ratio. The actual real exchange rate appreciated as it converged to the medium run NATREX. However, the rise in time preference has lowered the longer run value of the NATREX. The actual real effective exchange rate and the medium run NATREX exceed their long run values in the postunification period.

The deviations of the actual real effective exchange rate from the medium run NATREX are due to cyclical factors[52] and to short run capital flows. The latter result from anticipations of nominal interest rates in Germany and the US. These short run effects have expectations of zero, they do produce significant deviations from the NATREX, and their effects may take some time to disappear.

Appendix: Econometrics[53]

The econometrics are concerned with the estimation of equation (15) in the text, $R(t) = BZ(t) + b[R(t-1) - BZ(t-1)] + e(t)$, by nonlinear least squares. The definitions of the variables are in the section on the data. The dependent variable, the real effective exchange rate (GRREU), is integrated $I(1)$ and not stationary. The variables Z contain time preference, the q-ratio, capacity utilization and a dummy for pre and post unification.

A four quarter moving average of the q-ratio (MAQRATIO) is integrated $I(1)$ and is not stationary. In table A1, the time preference variable refers to a four

---

[52] The capacity utilization rate was not a significant variable in explaining the real exchange rate in the appendix tables. However, it was most informative to compare the q-ratio with its cyclically adjusted value in explaining the effects of German unification.

[53] The paper by Lim in this issue discusses how the econometrics should be done.

Table A1. NLS // Dependent Variable is GRREU

Sample: 1975:2–1993:3
Included observations: 74 after adjusting endpoints
Convergence achieved after 22 iterations

GRREU = $C(1) + C(2)$*MAQRATIO + $C(3)$*MAGRQGOV + $C(4)$*MAGRCUR
$\quad\quad + C(5)$*(GRREU(-1) $- C(1) - C(2)$*MAQRATIO(-1) $- C(3)$*MAGRQGOV
$\quad\quad - C(4)$*MAGRCUR(-1)) $+ C(6)$*DUM

	Coefficient	Std. Error	T-Statistic	Prob.
$C(1)$	222.7224	43.11246	5.166080	0.0000
$C(2)$	15.07066	6.255311	2.409259	0.0187
$C(3)$	−687.0463	172.7639	−3.976794	0.0002
$C(4)$	−0.106351	0.193021	−0.550984	0.5835
$C(5)$	0.901645	0.049591	18.18144	0.0000
$C(6)$	2.162662	0.713718	3.030136	0.0035

R-squared	0.963734	Mean dependent var	88.61946
Adjusted R-squared	0.961068	S.D. dependent var	8.840537
S.E. of regression	1.744354	Akaike info criterion	1.190373
Sum squared resid	206.9084	Schwartz criterion	1.377189
Log likelihood	−143.0453	F-statistic	361.4083
Durbin-Watson stat	1.628354	Prob (F-statistic)	0.000000

quarter moving average government time preference in unified Germany (MAGRQGOV). In table A2, the time preference variable refers to a four quarter moving average social time preference, public plus private, in unified Germany (MAGRQCON). A capacity utilization rate variable (MAGRCUR), is a four quarter moving average of the rate of capacity utilization in manufacturing. A dummy variable DUM was used to separate preunification (equal to zero), and post unification (equal to one). The sample period is from 1975:2 to 1993:4, due to the use of four quarter moving averages.

In both tables, time preference depreciates, the q-ratio appreciates the long run real exchange rate. The unification dummy is significant and the capacity utilization rate is not significant.

In table A1, which uses *government* time preference, the deviation between the actual real effective exchange GRREU(t) rate and the estimated value $BZ(t)$ over the entire sample period is called error1. There is one cointegrating equation, using the Johansen test. For the period prior to unification, 1975:2–1990:3, error1 is stationary. The ADF(N, 2) $= -2.33$ is significant at the 5% level. For the entire period, 1975:2–1993:3, it is not stationary. The ADF(N, 2) $= -1.45$. The (N, 2) means that no constant was used and there were two lags.

Table A2. NLS // Dependent Variable is GRREU

Sample: 1975:2–1993:3
Included observations: 74 after adjusting endpoints
Converge achieved after 5 iterations

GRREU = $C(1) + C(2)$*MAQRATIO + $C(3)$*MAGRQCON + $C(4)$*MAGRCUR
    $+ C(5)$*(GRREU(-1) $- C(1) - C(2)$*MAQRATIO(-1) $- C(3)$*MAGRQCON
    $- C(4)$*MAGRCUR(-1)) $+ C(6)$*DUM

	Coefficient	Std. Error	t-Statistic	Prob.
$C(1)$	357.3721	65.25078	5.476902	0.0000
$C(2)$	11.38278	5.849916	1.945801	0.0558
$C(3)$	−342.8246	73.52306	−4.662818	0.0000
$C(4)$	−0.187748	0.186709	−1.005564	0.3182
$C(5)$	0.863759	0.049974	17.28409	0.0000
$C(6)$	3.262121	0.933255	3.495425	0.0008

R-squared	0.966600	Mean dependent var	88.61946
Adjusted R-squared	0.964144	S.D. dependent var	8.840537
S.E. of regression	1.674022	Akaike info criterion	1.108063
Sum squared resid	190.5598	Schwartz criterion	1.294879
Log likelihood	−139.9998	F-statistic	393.5814
Durbin-Watson stat	1.719678	Prob (F-statistic)	0.000000

In table A1, we perform the tests on the error $e(t) = R(t) - \{BZ(t) + b[R(t-1) - BZ(t-1)]\}$ from the entire equation. The error is stationary. The Breusch-Godfrey serial correlation LM test yields an $F = 1.29$ with a probability of 0.28. Hence there is no serial correlation of errors. The ARCH test yields an $F = 1.92$ with a probability of 0.15. Hence there is no heteroskedasticity. The errors are normal: the Jarque-Bera statistic is 1.5 with a probability of 0.46.

In table A2, which uses *social* time preference MAGRQCON, the results are similar. Define error2 as the deviation (GRREU$(t) - BZ(t)$), where the estimates of B are in table A2. The graph of BZ is called NATREXG1 in figure 7. For the period prior to unification, 1975:1–1990:3, the error2 is stationary. The ADF$(N, 2) = -3.27$, which is significant at the 5% level. For the entire period, 1975:1–1993:3, the error2 is not stationary. The ADF$(N, 2) = -0.99$. This difference is apparent in figure 7 for the postunification period, where the nonstationary error2 is the deviation between the rising real exchange rate GRREU and the declining NATREXG1.

The NLS estimate of the entire equation is GRREUF in figure 7. The residual from the entire equation $R(t) - \{BZ(t) + b[R(t-1) - BZ(t-1)]\} = e(t) = $ GRREU $-$ GRREUF), is stationary. This can be seen from figure 7 by comparing the actual real exchange rate GRREU with GRREUF.

There is no serial correlation of the error from the entire equation. The Breusch-Godfrey F-statistic in the LM test, with two lags, is 0.759 with a probability of 0.47. The ARCH test yields an F-statistic 0.29 with a probability of 0.34. Hence there is no heteroskedasticity. Therefore the NLS has produced efficient estimates.

References

Allen PR (1995) The Economic and Policy Implications of the NATREX Approach. In: Stein JL, Allen PR: Fundamental Determinants of Exchange Rates. Oxford University Press, Oxford, ch. 1

Bayoumi T et al. (1994) The Robustness of Equilibrium Exchange Rate Calculations to Alternative Assumptions and Methodologies. In: Willaimson J (ed) Equilibrium Exchange rates. Institute for International Economics, Washington, DC

Breuer JB (1994) An Assessment of the Evidence on Purchasing Power Parity. In: Williamson J (ed) Equilibrium Exchange rates. Institute for International Economics, Washington, DC

Clark P (1995) Concepts of Equilibrium Exchange Rates. JOICE, this issue

Clausen V, Willms M (1994) Lessons from German Monetary Union for European Monetary Union. Journal of international and Comparative economics 3/3:195–228

Crouhy-Veyrac L, Saint Marc M (1995) The French Franc and the Deutsche Mark, 1971–1990. In: Stein JL, Allen PR: Fundamental Determinants of Exchange Rates. Oxford University Press, Oxford, ch. 4

Friedmann W, Hermann H (1994) A Review of Gerlinde and Hans-Werner Sinn: Jumpstart. Journal of international and Comparative economics 3

Infante EF, Stein JL (1973) Optimal Growth with Robust Feedback Control. Review of Economic Studies XL (1):47–60

Lim GC (1995) The Econometrics of Cointegration. JOICE, this issue

Masson PR, Kremers J, Horne J (1993) Net Foreign Assets and International Adjustment. International Monetary Fund, Working paper 93/33

Nurkse R (1945) Conditions of International Monetary Equilibrium, Essays in International Finance. International Finance Section, Princeton University

Obstfeld M, Rogoff K (1995) The Intertemporal Approach to the Current Account. In: Grossman G, Rogoff K (eds) Handbook of International Economics 3. North Holland, Amsterdam

Rogoff K (1992) Traded Goods Consumption Smoothing and the Random Walk Behavior of the Real Exchange Rate. Bank of Japan, Monetary and Economic Studies 10(2)

Sauernheimer K, Grassinger R (1995) The Long Run Determinants of the real Exchange Rate, The Case of Germany. University of Munich, Working Paper

Sinn G, Sinn H-W (1992) Jumpstart: The Economic Unification of Germany. MIT Press

Stein JL (1994) The Natural Real Exchange Rate of the United States Dollar and Determinants of Capital Flows. In: Williamson J (ed) Equilibrium Exchange rates. Institute for International Economics, Washington, DC

Stein JL (1995) The Fundamental Determinants of the Real Exchange Rate of the US Dollar Relative to the G7. International Monetary Fund Working Paper 95/81, IMF, Washington, DC

Stein JL (1990) The Real Exchange Rate. Journal of Banking and Finance, Special Issue on Real and Nominal Exchange Rates 14/5

Stein JL, Reynolds Allen P et al. (1995) Fundamental Determinants of Exchange Rates. Oxford University Press

Williamson J (1994) Introduction chapter 1 and Estimates of FEERS chapter 6. In: Williamson J (ed) Equilibrium Exchange rates. Institute for International Economics, Washington, DC

Concepts of Equilibrium Exchange Rates

PETER B. CLARK[1]

Research Department, International Monetary Fund, Washington DC, USA

Abstract

Calculations of estimated equilibrium exchange rates can provide guidance in judging the extent to which actual exchange rates are in line with the fundamentals. First, we describe the concepts of Williamson's FEER and the IMF economists' DEER equilibrium exchange rate. Then these concepts are contrasted with the NATREX approach. Finally, we suggest a way of combining these approaches.

Ever since the shift in 1973 from pegged to managed floating exchange rates among the industrial countries, there has been concern with the increased volatility of both nominal and real exchange rates. One approach to reduce this volatility is reflected in the target zone literature popularized by John Williamson, who also introduced the concept of the "fundamental equilibrium exchange rate" or FEER as the anchor for the target zone.[2] The shift in exchange rate regime also prompted the International Monetary Fund to alter its Articles of Agreement to give particular prominence to surveillance by the Fund over the international monetary system and over members' exchange rate policies. The exercise of this surveillance responsibility necessarily involves an assessment of members' exchange rates in terms of their consistency with economic fundamentals.[3] In light of the large fluctuations in exchange rates over the floating rate period, calculations of estimated equilibrium exchange rates can provide some guidance in judging the

---

[1] The author is an Assistant Director in the Research Department of the International Monetary Fund. He is indebted to Jerome Stein for his encouragement to write this note and for stimulating discussions on this topic. The views expressed are those of the author and do not necessarily reflect those of the staff or the Board of the IMF.

[2] For his most recent and most comprehensive presentation of FEERs, see his chapter, "Estimates of FEERs," in Williamson (1994).

[3] For a discussion of methods for assessing whether exchange rates are broadly in line with economic fundamentals, see Clark et al., 1994.

extent to which actual exchange rates are in line with economic fundamentals. Finally, in this issue of *JOICE,* the paper by Stein and Sauernheimer on "The Real Exchange Rates of Germany" develops an exchange rate concept in some respects related to the FEER which they call the NATREX (natural real exchange rate).

Given the clear interest in exchange rates from a policy perspective, as well as the ongoing challenge to economists to explain and understand exchange rate movements, it is timely to take stock of some of these different concepts of exchange rates with a view to clarifying their relationships and to suggesting ways that they might be adapted and improved. This note first briefly describes the FEER and the closely related concept of the DEER recently applied by a group of economists at the Fund in Bayoumi et al. (1994). The distinguishing characteristic of this approach is the calculation of a real exchange rate that purports to be consistent with internal and external balance. It then contrasts the DEER with the NATREX approach to equilibrium exchange rates which involves the explicit modeling of the actual exchange rate. Finally, it suggests a possible way of combining certain key aspects of both approaches which in principle could have distinct advantages in providing a measure of the equilibrium exchange rate for use as a benchmark against which to assess actual exchange rates.

The FEER/DEER exchange rate concept is based on the basic notion of macroeconomic balance which has both an internal and external dimension. Internal balance is identified as the level of output consistent with both full employment, i.e., with the economy operating at capacity output, and a low sustainable rate of inflation. Thus internal balance is closely connected to the concept of macroeconomic stability, and in particular with the level of unemployment consistent with a nonaccelerating rate of inflation (NAIRU). The idea is to abstract from short-run cyclical conditions and temporary factors and focus on the "economic fundamentals," i.e., the underlying conditions that are likely to persist over the medium term. These conditions are not necessarily those projected to occur in the future, but rather are desirable outcomes that may in fact never be realized. In this sense, the FEER exchange rate measure is a normative one, as Williamson has rightly acknowledged (see Williamson (1994), pp. 180–181). Indeed, he characterizes the FEER as the equilibrium exchange rate that would be consistent "ideal macroeconomic performance." It is for this reason that Bayoumi et al. refer to their exchange rate measure as the "desired" equilibrium exchange rate (DEER), i.e., consistent with desired positions of internal and external balance. But this normative aspect by itself is not a criticism of the approach, as it simply reflects the need to calibrate the exchange rate at a set of well-defined economic conditions. One could, of course, choose a different set of conditions at which to calculate the exchange rate, e.g., those most likely to prevail over the period of interest, which need not correspond to those identified as "desirable."

This point can be made more formally by expressing the real exchange rate, E, as a function of a set of economic fundamentals, $X_1, \ldots, X_n$, and a set of transitory factors, $T_1, \ldots, T_n$. Abstracting from dynamic effects so that time subscripts can be avoided, and allowing for a random disturbance term or unexplained residual, e, the actual exchange rate (domestic prices divided by foreign prices, both expressed in a numeraire) can be represented as:

$$E = a_1 X_1 + \ldots + a_n X_n + b_1 T_1 + \ldots + b_n T_n + e. \tag{1}$$

In equation (1) the actual real exchange rate is exhaustively explained by economic fundamentals, transitory factors, and a random disturbance. The FEER/DEER concept has two distinct characteristics in terms of equation (1): the transitory factors are explicitly excluded, as they are not germane to the analysis, and the values of the fundamentals are put at their desired levels. With the latter denoted by a bar over the variable, the FEER is given by:

$$\text{FEER} = a_1 \bar{X}_1 + \ldots a_n \bar{X}_n. \tag{2}$$

The equation used to calculate the FEER/DEER is not as general as (2). Rather, it is based on an equation (or set of equations) that determines the current account. This is given by equation (3), where A is the level of domestic demand (absorption) and the subscripts d and f denote domestic and foreign, respectively.

$$\text{CA} = \text{CA}(A_d, A_f, E) \qquad CA_1 < 0, \ CA_2 > 0, \ CA_3 < 0. \tag{3}$$

This is basically an equation explaining the current account in terms of domestic and foreign absorption and the real exchange rate. To calculate the FEER from (3) one needs the levels of domestic and foreign absorption that are consistent with full employment as well as the current account position that is regarded as desirable. Solving (3) for the FEER gives:

$$\text{FEER} = F(\overline{CA}, \bar{A}_d, \bar{A}_f). \tag{4}$$

Thus for levels of foreign and domestic absorption that are consistent with capacity output, the FEER is computed as that level of the real exchange rate that will achieve the exogenously given desired current account.

Implicit in this approach is that the current account calibrated at full employment provides an appropriate guide or benchmark as to where the exchange rate should move over the medium term. However, this approach does not involve any explicit theory of exchange rate determination. In particular, factors that affect the capital account are not taken into account in determining the FEER. However, as Williamson notes, capital account considerations may well have a role to play in coming to a view as to the desirable current account position and would therefore enter the calculation in this way. Nonetheless, it remains the case that the behavior of asset holders, in terms of their choices regarding investment in foreign versus domestic assets, is not taken into account in any systematic fashion and therefore these capital account considerations are assumed not to affect the real exchange rate over the medium term.

Moreover, the empirical applications of this approach do not rely on the estimation of a relationship between the real exchange rate and its determinants. Rather, they rely on the estimation of a current account model to identify a statistically robust relationship between the real exchange rate and the current account. Thus there appears to be an implicit assumption that over the medium term the real exchange rate is determined by the current account.

By contrast, the other main strand of literature dealing with equilibrium exchange rates involves the specification and estimation of an equation that explains the actual movement of the real exchange in terms of changes in economic fundamentals. This approach involves the use of equation (1), where differences in implementation involve the extent to which transitory factors are omitted and fundamental factors are calibrated at desired levels.[4] Some of those pursuing this approach (Faruqee and Stein) take explicit account of capital flows and endogenize the capital account, whereas others (Edwards and Elbadawi) treat them as exogenous. These two different types of analysis are briefly described in turn.

Both Faruqee and Stein take as their starting point the balance-of-payments equation which equates the current account with the capital account. Stein's specification of the NATREX abstracts from short-term capital flows, which are assumed to have an expected value of zero, and concentrates only on long-term portfolio and direct investment flows, which together are referred to as nonspeculative capital flows. These net flows are determined by the difference between national saving and investment. Thus the capital account is determined by desired saving, which in turn is a function of the rate of time preference, and desired investment, which is determined by the Tobin q ratio. In the NATREX, two basic variables – productivity and thrift – drive the capital account, which in turn influences the real exchange rate through changes in the current account. Moreover, the model also takes into account stock equilibrium conditions, so that the steady state is reached when the domestic capital stock and net foreign assets are at their long-term values. In the steady state, the real exchange rate, the capital stock, and the level of net foreign assets are all functions of the exogenous foreign and domestic productivity and thrift variables.

The distinction between current and capital accounts is also drawn sharply by Faruqee. In his illustrative model, the current account balance is the sum of the trade balance, which is a function of the real exchange rate and exogenous variables (X), and interest income received (or paid) on a country's net foreign asset (or debt) position, F:

$$CA = cE + X + rF \qquad c < 0, \ r = \text{domestic real interest rate} \qquad (5)$$

---

[4] These approaches include Edwards (1994), Elbadawi (1994), Faruqee (1994), and Stein (1994, 1995a, 1995b).

Faruqee points out that a viable balance of payments position requires that the current account be financed by a desired or sustainable level of capital flows. In his model, he posits that the desired rate of net foreign asset accumulation (or decumulation), which corresponds to the desired rate of net national saving, is given by:

$$KA^d = d(r - r^*) + f(F^d - F), \qquad d < 0, \ f > 0 \tag{6}$$

where:

$KD^d =$ desired net capital outflow

$r^* \quad =$ world real interest rate

$F^d \quad =$ target or desired level of net foreign assets.

Combining equations (5) and (6) gives the full balance of payments equation:

$$cZ + X + rF = d(r - r^*) + f(F^d - F). \tag{7}$$

This balance of payments equation requires that the desired excess income over spending be equal to the desired net change in claims on foreigners. In Faruqee's model, the actual real exchange rate can be solved as a function of the long-run value, $\bar{Z}$ and the difference between the actual and the long-run stock equilibrium level of net foreign assets, $\bar{F}$:

$$Z_t = \bar{Z}_t + s(F_t - \bar{F}_t) \qquad s > 0. \tag{8}$$

The solution for $\bar{Z}_t$ is given by:

$$\bar{Z}_t = (r/c)\bar{F}_t + \frac{1}{c}\bar{X}_t \tag{9}$$

The NATREX model and that of Faruqee share a number of common features. First, the real exchange rate responds to the difference between the actual and long-term desired level of net foreign assets, as shown in (8). This can be referred to as the short-run equilibrium level of the real exchange rate. Second, the long run equilibrium level, as shown in equation (9), is a function of both factors affecting the capital account, $\bar{F}$, as well as those affecting the current account, $\bar{X}$. Third, in both models the issue of a sustainable or desirable current account position does not arise. Agents are always at the desired positions, whether this be in the short run or the long run. Basically, the real exchange rate and the real interest rate adjust so that the current account balance is willingly financed by wealth holders.

However, there are some significant differences in empirical implementation. Faruqee makes no attempt to deal with issues of internal or, as noted above, external balance. Using cointegration analysis, he estimates basically equation (9) using productivity growth differentials, the relative price of non-traded goods, and the terms of trade as variables determining the current account (the X variable), and treats the actual stock of net foreign assets as an exogenous variable. This approach has no normative elements, as he simply tries to explain the (annual average) real effective value of the yen and the U.S. dollar in terms of the economic fundamentals, and refers to the fitted value of the real exchange rate from his estimating equation as the "trend" value, rather than equilibrium value.

Stein's approach is similar to Faruqee's in that it does not always involve a normative statement about what is a desirable or sustainable current account. Rather, the change in net foreign assets reflects the preferences of wealth holders to save and invest, and to invest more or less of their wealth in foreign assets. However, Stein claims that his approach does provide an estimate of the real exchange rate that is consistent with internal balance and in this sense his analysis has a normative element.

However, in the earlier version of the paper in this volume on the real value of the deutsche mark, Stein appears to argue that the NATREX provides a good representation of the real value of the deutsche mark when the German economy is in a position of internal and external balance, i.e., the NATREX is the level of the real exchange rate which is consistent with the German economy being at a desired and sustainable domestic as well as external position. One aspect of this question relates to measurement issues. The authors have made cyclical adjustments to the variables in the model, but these adjustments are not the same for all variables. For example, a Hodrick-Prescott filter is used for the real exchange rate, but a four-quarter moving average is used for the current account. Presumably, the same method should be used for all variables. Second, there is a fairly well-established notion of potential output that corresponds to unemployment being at the NAIRU level. By contrast, the NATREX, which involves only a cyclical adjustment of the actual exchange rate and other variables, need not correspond to the level of the exchange rate when the economy is at capacity output.[5] Third, the notion of external balance, which is admittedly more problematic, remains rather vague in the paper. The authors appear to imply that the value of the current account that reflects underlying investment and saving behavior constitutes a position of external balance. This approach seems to be incomplete in that no attention is given to whether the fiscal position is sustainable and whether the external balance reflects an undesirable or inappropriate fiscal stance. Moreover, the assessment of the external balance needs to be supplemented by consideration of stock

---

[5] For a more extensive discussion of this point, see the article by Stanley Black, "On the Concept and Usefulness of the Equilibrium Rate of Exchange," chapter 8 in Williamson (1994).

equilibrium, e.g., whether it implies that the level of net foreign assets is changing at an unsustainable rate. Finally, the empirically estimated NATREX follows the actual real exchange rate extremely well, and therefore there does not appear to be much scope for departures from internal and external equilibrium in the empirical results of the authors.

One alternative worth pursuing would combine an estimation approach similar to that in the Stein and Sauernheimer paper with an externally-derived estimate of internal balance, and which would therefore involve both positive and normative elements. The normative element would be estimates of potential output for Germany as well as her major trading partners. The estimation would be done using data that had been adjusted for seasonal but not for cyclical fluctuations. Departures of actual from potential output could then be incorporated in the estimated error correction equation for both the exchange rate and the current account. The exchange rate corresponding to internal balance could in principle be computed from the estimated coefficient and the magnitude of the gap between actual and potential output. In long-run equilibrium, output would be equal to potential and the exchange rate would reflect only the underlying fundamentals of productivity and thrift. The basic point is that departures from potential output over the cycle need to be identified and taken into account in a systematic fashion.

The papers by Edwards and Elbadawi mentioned above attempt to combine both positive and normative elements in an integrated manner. The positive element embodies the approach pursued by Faruqee and Stein, namely, the specification and estimation of an equation explaining the real exchange rate in terms of economic fundamentals, such as the terms of trade, technical change, level of tariffs, government consumption of nontradeables, and an exogenous measure of capital flows. To try to calibrate the model at a position that bears some resemblance to internal balance, Edwards introduces into the dynamic equation for the real exchange rate what he calls measures of "inconsistent policies." Albadawi, on the other hand, estimates the permanent or sustainable components of the fundamentals by using the time series techniques introduced by Beveridge and Nelson. While these may have some value in eliminating transitory developments, they do not appear capable of calibrating the model at a position of internal balance as is done in the FEER/DEER approach.

The upshot of this note is that there remains a gap between the two strands of literature on equilibrium exchange rates. The FEER/DEER approach has the advantage that it clearly specifies the conditions at which the exchange rate can be calibrated, with the calculated value of the real exchange rate then used as a benchmark to assess the appropriateness of the actual market-determined rate. It has the disadvantage, however, of not being based on a clearly defined, and empirically implemented, approach to exchange rate determination. On the other hand, the approaches that attempt to explain empirically the market-determined real exchange rate generate results that do not provide direct guidance to the policymaker for the assessment of exchange rates. Thus there remains considerable work to be done to narrow this gap.

References

Bayoumi T et al. (1994) The Robustness of Equilibrium Exchange Rate Calculations to Alternative Assumptions and Methodologies. Chapter 2 in Williamson

Clark P et al. (1994) Exchange Rates and Economic Fundamentals. IMF Occasional Paper No 116. International Monetary Fund, Washington

Edwards S (1994) Real and Monetary Determinants of Real Exchange Rate Behavior: Theory and Evidence from Developing Countries. Chapter 3 in Williamson

Elbadawi I (1994) Estimating Long-Run Equilibrium Real Exchange Rates. Chapter 4 in Williamson

Faruquee H (1995) Long-Run Determinant of the Real Exchange Rate: A Stock Flow Perspective. Staff Papers, International Monetary Fund 42/1

Williamson J (ed) (1994) Estimating Equilibrium Exchange Rates. Institute for International Economics, Washington

Stein JL (1994) The Natural Real Exchange Rate of the U.S. Dollar and Determinants of Capital Flows. Chapter 5 in Williamson

Stein JL (1995) The Fundamental Determinants of the Real Exchange Rate of the U.S. Dollar Relative to other G-7 Currencies forthcoming Working Paper. International Monetary Fund, Washington

Stein JL, Sauernheimer K (1995) The Real Exchange Rates of Germany. This volume

A Note on Estimating Dynamic Economic Models of the Real Exchange Rate

G. C. LIM

Department of Economics, University of Melbourne, Parkville, Victoria 3052, Australia

Abstract

This note explains why the econometric techniques for dealing with non-stationary data are typically: first, unit root tests to establish the order of integration; second, Johansen tests to determine the number of cointegrating vector; third, two types of residual diagnostic tests to ensure that the parameters are consistently and efficiently estimated.

This note is a revised version of my comments on the paper Stein and Sauernheimer (hereafter SS) presented at the CIDEI conference. It contains those sections of my original comments which deal with the estimation and testing of a dynamic economic model of the type proposed by SS using cointegration techniques.[1]

The aim of the empirical analysis conducted by SS is to test the real exchange rate (here denoted by R) is significantly affected by fundamental determinants (here represented by vector Z). The economic theory supporting the dynamic model is influenced by three considerations: (1) that the real exchange rate (R) is a non-stationary $I(1)$ variable; (2) that R is affected by fundamental determinants (Z), also found to be non-stationary; and (3) that these shocks (Z) have permanent effects on R. It follow that since R and Z are hypothesised to have a long run relationship, that the model should be tested using cointegration techniques.[2]

In applying econometric techniques for non-stationary data, the following steps are typically followed. First, unit root tests are conducted to establish the

---

[1] The original comments are published in CIDEI working paper, 1994. While the issues discussed in this note arose originally with the version of the SS paper presented at the Conference, they are by no means unique. In this note, the comments have been slighty revised to place the econometric issues in a broader context. I am grateful to the editor and the organisers of the Conference for this opportunity.

[2] The dynamics underlying the long-run relationship between R and Z involves three phases: an impact phase (the effect of Z on R, holding foreign debt and acpital constant), and intermediate phase (when R changes as a result of induced changes in the current account and capital accumulation), and a final phase (when R stabilises at a level where the trade balance equals the interest payments).

order of integration of the variables hypothesised to have a relationship; second, Johansen tests are applied to determine the number of cointegrating vector amongst the $I(1)$ variables; and third, the cointegrating parameters are estimated.[3]

A number of cointegrating estimators exist today to generate consistent estimates.[4] However, not all cointegration estimators produce efficient estimates, a necessary condition if the t-statistics are to be used to facilitate significance testing of the variables. The conditions under which different cointegration estimators result in consistent and efficient parameters seem to be less well-known, leading to potential misuse and misinterpretation of results. A case in point is the use of the OLS estimator to estimate dynamic models with $I(1)$ variables.[5] The problem here, lies not with the use of the OLS estimator *per se* (because it will produce consistent estimates) but with the use of the OLS generated t-statistics for statistical inference.

The aim of this note is to use simple examples to show why the OLS estimator is not efficient for estimating dynamic models with $I(1)$ variables. Two associated issues will also be discussed. They are the role of two types of residual diagnostic tests, and the sense in which the cointegrating vector represent long run effects.[6] The following sections are devoted to discussing the choice of estimator, the role of residual diagnostic testing and the interpretation of the cointegrating vector. In keeping with the simple examples, reference is made only to regression based least squares cointegrating estimators.[7]

Estimating a Dynamic Model with $I(1)$ Variables

Consider the following econometric model, represented by equations (1) and (2) below,

$$Z_t = \mu_{1t} \tag{1}$$

$$R_t = \beta Z_t + \mu_{2t} \tag{2}$$

where μ_{1t} and μ_{2t} are white noise terms.

---

[3] For an introduction to the cointegration literature, see and Dickey, Jansen and Thornton (1991) and Perman (1991).

[4] See, for example the estimators proposed in Engle and Granger (1987), Phillips and Hansen (1990), Phillips and Loreton (1991) and Saikkonen (1991).

[5] See, the version of the SS paper presented at the Conference, CIDEI Working Paper 1994.

[6] The three issues selected for discussion – the misuse of the OLS t-statistics for statistical inference, the lack of diagnostic testing and the misinterpretation of the cointegrating vector as medium run partial effects – are derived from the original SS paper.

[7] As distinct from, for example Johansen (1988) and Phillips (1991) system estimators.

In this example, Z are pure exogenous shocks (equation 1) which affect the real exchange rate R (equation 2). Under these assumptions, estimating equation (2) by OLS will produce consistent and efficient estimates of β since both Z and R are $I(0)$ terms and moreover, the residuals in (2) are white noise terms.

However, the dynamic economic model presented by SS is based on the fact that R and Z and $I(1)$ variables. Hence the econometric model needs to be altered to capture these stylised facts. Dynamics may be introduced into the econometric model above by allowing for two simple autoregressive structures; one on the shock terms Z and one through the dynamic adjustment of R. The model becomes

$$R_t = \beta Z_t + \mu_{2t} \tag{2}$$

$$Z_t = Z_{t-1} + \varepsilon_{1t} \tag{3}$$

$$\mu_{2t} = \mu_{2t-1} + \varepsilon_{2t} \tag{4}$$

where ε_{1t} and ε_{2t} are now the white noise terms.

Incorporating (3) and (4) into (2), obtain the generating process for R as (5) or (5'),

$$R_t = \beta Z_t + (R - \beta Z)_{t-1} + \varepsilon_{2t} \tag{5}$$

$$R_t = R_{t-1} + \beta \varepsilon_{1t} + \varepsilon_{2t} \tag{5'}$$

From (3) and (5'), note that both Z and R are now $I(1)$ variables with cointegrating vector β. However, in this case, β should not be estimated by OLS because note, from equation (5), that the residual structure is of the form $(\mu_{2t-1} + \varepsilon_{2t})$. These residuals may be $I(0)$, but they will also be autocorrelated. Hence, OLS estimates will not be efficient, and the t-statistics will not be reliable for statistical inference.

The correct cointegration estimator (i.e., one that generates consistent and efficient estimates) depends on the data generating process of the variables.[8] For example, in the case where the data generating process of R and Z are as described in equations (2) and (3) respectively, the cointegrating vector β can be consistently and efficiently estimated from equation (5) using non-linear least squares.

Diagnostic Tests of Residuals

However, data generating processes of variables are generally unknown. Consequently, in practice, diagnostic tests of the residuals have to be conducted to check

---

[8] For more details on this issue see, for example Banerjee and Hendry (1992), Ericsson (1992) and Lim and Martin (1994).

that an appropriate estimator have been used to generate consistent and efficient estimates. The rationale for these residual tests may be seen with reference to the example above. If, for example, R and Z are correctly described, then estimating equation (5) by non-linear least squares would produce estimates of the cointegrating vector β as well as regression residual which are white noise. Thus, it follows that two types of diagnostic tests of residuals would help establish that consistent and efficient cointegrating estimates have been produced. They are: (1) tests to establish that the relationship between R and Z is cointegrated and not spurious, and (2) tests to establish that the regression residuals, are white noise terms. For the former, perform unit root tests on the residuals of the long run equation $(R_t - \hat{\beta} Z_t)$,[9] and for the latter, perform diagnostic tests (such as for autocorrelation, heteroscedasticity, ARCH, non-normality) on the regression residuals (that is, ε_{2t}). If both these tests are satisfied, then the regression generated t-statistics can be used for testing the significance of the Z variables and inference can be made as to whether the cointegration results represent significant long run effects.

Interpretation of the Cointegrating Vector

Another issue that arose with the appplication of cointegration is the sense in which the cointegrating vector captures long-run effects. To illustrate the interpretation of the cointegrating vector in a simple way, consider the generalisation of equation (5) into a dynamic economic model represented as distributed-lag equation (6),

$$R_t = \alpha R_{t-1} + \beta_1 Z_t + \beta_2 Z_{t-1} + v_t \tag{6}$$

where v_t is a white noise term.

Rewrite (6) using the long-run steady state result $R = \left(\dfrac{\beta_1 + \beta_2}{1 - \alpha} \right) Z,$

$$R_t = \beta Z_t + \alpha (R_{t-1} - \beta Z_{t-1}) - \left(\frac{\alpha \beta_1 + \beta_2}{1 - \alpha} \right) \Delta Z_t + v_t, \tag{7}$$

where $\beta = \left(\dfrac{\beta_1 + \beta_2}{1 - \alpha} \right)$.

The format of equation (7) is particularly useful for this case study because it contains the three terms typically found in regression based cointegration analysis

---

[9] Note, as an aside, that residual tests are needed even if the Johansen tests for determining the number of cointegrating vector(s) between R and Z, indicate the presence of only one cointegrating vector. It could be that only one of the Z variables is significant, a result which cannot be infered from the Johansen tests since they are not designed to determine significance.

and helps highlight the problem with OLS estimation and with the interpretation of the cointegrating vector. The first term describes the long-run relationship between the variables R and Z, the second term is the error-correction component, and the third term captures the impact effect of a change in Z on the real exchange rate. Equation (7) clearly shows that OLS will generate consistent and efficient estimates when the underlying model is static (that is, when $\alpha = \beta_2 = 0$). More importantly is also highlights the interpretation of the estimated coefficients between R and the Z variables; the β coefficient are viewed as steady-state long run values because these coefficients capture the total, not partial, effects of the shock Z on R.

Equation (7) may also be used to reiterate the point made previously about estimation and residual testing. In the case, where the "true" reduced form model is correctly represented by equation (6), the cointegrating vector β would be consistently and efficiently estimated from equation (7), which contains three terms. Using an estimator which ignores, for example the third term would result in inefficient estimates (except in the special case when $\beta_2 = -\alpha\beta_1$). Thus the point is made, again, that from an applied point of view, since true underlying data generating processes are unknown, it is important to perform diagnostic tests of the residuals.

In conclusion, the aim of this note is to use simple examples to draw attention to certain aspects of the empirical analysis (estimation, inference and interpretation) of a dynamic model of the real exchange rate using cointegration techniques. To the extent that the SS model is a dynamic model based on non-stationary variables, the OLS is not the appropriate technique as the method fails to allow for the dynamic structure. Dynamic economic models require dynamic econometric techniques (such as the non-linear estimation model above) to generate consistent and efficient estimates. However, since data generating processes are unknown, it is important to conduct diagnostic tests on two sets of residuals (tests to confirm that the variables are cointegrated and tests to confirm that the regression residuals are white noise), to validate statistical inference based on t-statistics. Also, one final point, coefficients of the cointegrating vector are interpreted as long run results because they capture the total effects of the shock Z on R.

References

Banerjee A, Hendry DF (1992) Testing Integration and Cointegration. Special Issue of the Oxford Bulletin of Economics and Statistics 54/3

Dickey DA, Jansen DW, Thornton DL (1991) A Primer on Cointegration with an Application to Money and Income. Federal Reserve Bank of St. Louis Review 73/2:58–78

Engle RF, Granger CWJ (1987) Cointegration and Error Correction: Representation, Estimation and Testing. Econometrica 55/2:251–276

Ericsson NR (1992) Cointegration, Exogeneity and Policy Analysis: An Overview. Special Issue of the Journal of Policy Modelling 14/14:251–280

Johansen S (1988) Statistical Analysis of Cointegration Vectors. Journal of Economic Dynamics and Control 12/2:231–254

Lim GC, Martin VL (1994) Regression Based Cointegration Estimators with Applications. Journal of Economic Studies 22/1:3–22

Perman R (1991) Cointegration: An Introduction to the Literature. Journal of Economic Studies 18/3:3–29

Phillips PCB, Hansen BE (1990) Statistical Inference in Instrumental Variables Regression with $I(1)$ Processes. Review of Economic Studies 57/189:99–125

Phillips PCB (1991) Optimal Inference in Cointegrated Systems. Econometrica 59/2:283–306

Phillips PCB, Loreton M (1991) Estimating Long-Run Equilibria. Review of Economic Studies 58/195:407–436

Saikkonen P (1991) Asymptotically Efficient Estimation of Cointegrating Regressions. Econometric Theory 7/1:1–21

Trade Regimes and Gatt:
Resource Intensive vs. Knowledge Intensive Growth

GRACIELA CHICHILNISKY[1]

Program on Information and Resources and Department of Economics,
Columbia University, New York, N.Y. 10027

Abstract

Trading blocks can help or hinder the liberalization of world trade. A determining factor is whether trade within the block is organized around traditional comparative advantages, or around economies of scale.

Regional free trade agreements such as NAFTA can be a *substitutes* for global free trade when they are based on traditional comparative advantages; then each regional market develops market power and incentives to impose tariffs on the rest of the world. Alternatively, regional trade agreements can be *complementary* to global free trade. This occurs when the blocks are organized around the exploitation of economies of scale and based on knowledge-intensive sectors.

I establish that external economies of scale produce incentives for expanded trade; they can defeat the standard arguments for "optimal tariffs" and mitigate another negative feature of trading blocks: their tendency to divert trade from efficient to inefficient sources. The emergence of regional blocks organized around economies of scale can therefore lead to increasingly open international markets. I discuss policy implications for the EU and for free trade in the Americas.

1 The EU, NAFTA and the Gatt

Regional free trade zones have been unexpectedly successful in the last decade. Since 1980 the European Union enlarged significantly its membership and its

---

[1] Director, Program on Information and Resources, Professor of Economics, Columbia University, and 1994 Salinbemi Professor, University of Siena. E-mail: gc9@columbia.edu, fax: 2126780405, phone: 2126781148. First version: December 1992, revised September 1994. This article was orginally prepared for the United Nations Program of Trade Liberalization in the Americas, ECLAC, Washington D.C., and its results were the subject of an invited presentation at a U.N.-ECLA Conference on Trade Liberalization in the Americas, Washington D.C. June 1992, and at a Conference on "Globalization of Markets: Theoretical and empirical challenges and prospects for advances in research", organized by Centro Interdipartimenale di Economia International Universita di Roma "La Sapienza", Rome, October 27–28, 1994. I thank Kenneth Arrow, Geoffrey Heal, Jerome Stein, Ray Riezman and Alan Winters for valuable comments and suggestions. Research support from NSF Grants Nos. SBR-92-16028 and DMS 94-08798 and from the Sloan Foundation is acknowledged.

scope. Today the EU includes southern European countries, and it allows goods, people, services and capital to flow freely around an area accounting for about one fourth of world economic output.

In what appears to be a strategic response, the US has been activated to enter into similar agreements with its neighbors. The arithmetic is simple. The US accounted for about 40% of the world's output after the Second World War,[2] a figure that decreased steadily until today, when it represents about 25%. The recent completion of the European Union faced the US for the first time since 1945 with a unified group of countries that matches its own economic prowess. This changed matters: shortly afterwards a trade and investment agreement was signed with Canada followed almost immediately by the adoption of NAFTA. The agreement could expand to the rest of the Americas.

The same trend is observed in other regions. The six members of the Association of South East Asian Nations – Singapore, Malaysia, Thailand, Indonesia, the Philippines, and Brunei – have began in 1992 to build their Asean free trade area AFTA as a future counterweight to other international trading blocks. The Japanese have increasingly focused their economic attention in their own region, leading to more investment in and imports from the new East Asian manufacturing exporters. Even the Andean Pact seems to be progressing in Latin America after several decades of aimless discussions, with Mercosur following suit. Of the fourteen trading blocks in existence today[3] seven have been formed since 1992.

While regional free trade agreements prosper, the negotiations towards the liberalization of global trade have floundered for many years. The last round of Gatt negotiations, the Uruguay Round, was ratified recently by the US and also by the EU. All along the agricultural markets have been a key negotiating problem: this will be discussed later as an excellent example of the issues involved.

While the Gatt negotiations are political, it is reasonable to seek explanations for the situation from an economic viewpoint. The contrast between the lackluster performance of the Gatt and the success of the regional trade pacts raise disparate reactions. One view is that the emergence of regional trade pacts is a step in the right direction. "Custom unions", as regional free trade pacts are usually called, are in this view stepping stones towards world free trade. Another, quite distinct, reaction, is to fear that "customs unions" are inherently opposed to global free trade. Do custom unions increase free trade with insiders at the cost of diverting trade with outsiders?

---

[2] Before the Second World War the US represented about 25% of the world economy. This increased to 40% after the War due to the destruction of the German and Japanese economies.

[3] EU inaugurated in 1958, SEMAC in 1964, ASEAN in 1967, ANDEAN in 1969, CACM in 1974, ECOWAS in 1975, PTA in 1981, SADC in 1992, UEMOA in 1994, NAFTA in 1994, MERCOSUR in 1994/95, G3 in 1994/95, APEC in 1994 and VISEGRAD in 1994.

Since the classic works of Meade [21] and Viner [26], who classified the issues into trade creation and trade diversion, there has been little conceptual advance on this issue. But the issue is very alive today, and requires our attention.

This paper will re-examine the positive and negative aspects of trading blocks as they relate to gains from free trade. It is primarily a discussion of conceptual issues, although it is based on facts and on particular cases which are of interest to the trade liberalization in the Americas. I take a somewhat different approach to a familiar issue. Rather than asking the standard question of whether regional blocks help or hinder global free trade, I ask: *what type of trading block* is likely to lead to a trade war between the blocks, and what type is, instead, likely to expand global trade? In practical terms: what type of trade regimes within the blocks will provide economic incentives for expanding free trade?

I shall compare the impact on the world economy of trading blocks which are organized around two alternative principles, or trade regimes. One is *traditional comparative advantages,* the other is external *economies of scale.*[4] These represent two patterns of growth: resource-intensive vs. knowledge-intensive. The aim is to determine how the patterns of trade *inside* the blocks determine the trade relations *among* the blocks.

The paper has four parts. The first part reviews the existing economics of trading blocks, and uses this to explain the current situation in the EU and NAFTA. The second part presents a new conceptual approach focusing on the internal organization of the trading blocks and the economic incentives that this generates with respect to the rest of the world. The third part is a conclusion which pulls the arguments together for an evaluation of NAFTA, EU, and global free trade. The fourth part is an Appendix which provides a formal general equilibrium model of trading blocks, an extension of my model of North-South trade [4–6] which incorporates goods which are produced with external economies of scale. I establish rigorously in the Appendix the results which underlie the discussion in the text.

2 The Economics of Trading Blocks

International trade in the last ten years focussed on economic dynamics and on market imperfections. However the central tenet of the theory of international trade remains the same: the classic results on the efficiency of competitive markets.

In competitive markets, free trade leads to Pareto efficient allocations. There is no way to make a someone better off without making someone else worse off.

---

[4] I benefitted from the ideas of Jane Jacobs in "Cities and the Wealth of Nations", Random House, 1985.

Called the first theorem of welfare economics, the general result that competitive markets lead to efficient allocations seems to loom the larger, the more special cases of market imperfections are pointed out.

In view of the efficiency of competitive markets, the difficulties faced by Gatt in bringing an agreement about a world of free trade seems, at a first sight, irrational. It would appear that countries act as if they could, but prefer not to, achieve an efficient allocation. Indeed, some believe that the failure of Gatt is simply a version of the well-known prisoners' dilemma.[5]

Are countries irrational in evading free trade? Such a view would be incorrect. The Gatt's problems derive not from irrational behavior, not from a lack of coordination. There is a simple, rational explanation: while free trade in competitive markets leads to efficient solutions, when countries are large and have market power, this is no longer true. Free trade may not lead to Pareto efficient allocations when the countries are large and have market power. Indeed, large countries may choose the quantities they export in order to manipulate to their advantage world market prices, much the same way that a monopolist chooses to supply a quantity that maximizes its profits considering its impact on prices. Such strategies are rational for large countries. The only case where free trade leads surely to Pareto efficient allocations is when markets are competitive, when no country has market power.

Do all countries stand to gain from a move to free trade? The answer is negative. Under classical assumptions, a move from tariffs to free trade will typically make some countries better off but other countries worse off. It is true that if a competitive allocation were reached, it would be Pareto efficient. But in a world with tariffs, as we have today, under traditional assumptions some country will loose if free trade is adopted. There is therefore no reason for all countries to agree to free trade.

Indeed when countries are sufficiently large to have an impact on market prices, then they have an incentive to impose tariffs on each other. One may ask: precisely how do large countries benefit from protectionism? How do tariffs work?

Large countries can improve their position by improving their *terms of trade:* the prices of exports relative to those of imports. Better terms of trade means that the country pays less for what it buys, and receives more for what it sells. A country is typically better off with better terms of trade.

Of course, in competitive markets countries do not manipulate terms of trade to their advantage: this is practically the definition of competitive markets. But international trade theory proves that, under traditional assumptions, a large country does have an economic incentive to impose tariffs on others. This is the

---

[5] The words "prisoners' dilemma" are used to describe a generically inefficient situation, one which, with appropriate coordination between the players, can be altered so as to improve the welfare of all.

standard theorem on *optimal tariffs,* which is discussed in more detail below. The theorem says that, under traditional assumptions, there is always an *optimal tariff,* one at which the gains from increasing its terms of trade through tariffs exceeds the losses due to the attendant distortions. This theorem is widely accepted, understood and applied.

The argument in favor of optimal tariffs is of course not true for small countries. For this argument it is essential that the country should be large enough to have an impact on prices. Furthermore the larger the country, the more market power it has, and the more it can gain from imposing tariffs on others.

The importance of all this today is that if a world of small competitive economies merges into a few large trading blocks traditional, under traditonal assumptions, after the blocks are formed, there are more incentives for imposing tariffs than before. In other words, under traditional conditions, regional trade blocks, lead to protectionism.

The *optimal tariff* which we have just discussed is imposed by one country on others unilaterally. The classic theorem does not consider the possibility of retaliation by other countries. But what if they retaliate? What if other countries also impose tariffs in response?

We now move to a world of strategic considerations, a world with tariff wars. Each country imposes tariffs on each other, and does so strategically so as to maximize its welfare given the actions of others. The outcome of this tariff game was studied in Kennan and Riezman [15, 16]. If each country chooses as its tariff the best response to the others', a market equilibrium with tariffs is reached. We call this an *optimal tariff equilibrium* to distinguish it from the free trade equilibrium.[6]

In an optimal tariff equilibrium some countries are better of than they would be at a free trade equilibrium, [15, 16] and [25]. Furthermore, these works show that the larger the country, the more it can improve its welfare at the optimal tariff equilibrium.

To a certain extent the current situation in the world economy can be described as an optimal tariff equilibrium. Each country imposes tariffs on others strategically. In this light the difficulties of the Gatt have a reasonable explanation. The unwillingness of countries to agree to multilateral free trade is neither irrational nor a coordination problem. It is a rational response to economic incentives of countries with market power.

One immediate implication is that regional trade blocks will increase the market power of the market participants and therefore can lead to tariff wars. Under traditional conditions, the larger is the market power of a trade block, the larger is its incentive to impose tariffs on others. Even after retaliatory moves are

---

[6] It is not a competitive trade situation because the traders act strategically, manipulating prices. In a world with free and competitive trade, no-one has an impact on prices, nor does anyone act according to price strategies.

taken into account the same proposition holds: the larger the market power of the block, the greater its gains from a tariff war.

Since these results predict that regional free trade zones create incentives against global free trade under traditional assumptions, it is crucial to examine these assumptions closely. For whenever these conditions are satisfied, regional free trade inevitably leads to trade wars. And the larger the free trade zones, the more likely is that they will lead to trade wars.

I examine these conditions in the next section. This examination will be conceptual, but focused on particular cases of immediate interest. Recalling classical results on tariffs of A. Lerner [18] and of L. Metzler[23],[7] and based on new results on trading blocks with economies of scale of Chichilnisky [8] reported in the Appendix, I show that if the blocks are organized internally around the principle of economies of scale, the optimal tariff theorem can be defeated. *With increasing returns, a country may be better off with free trade than with tariffs.* Before I turn to the new results, I will explore the implications of the classic optimal tariff theorem on the European Union and on NAFTA.

NAFTA – and any further extension to a larger free trade zone in the Americas – emerged as a strategic response by the US to the creation of the European Union. The European Union is a free trade zone with a quarter of world output. In seeking to form a trading block with its natural trading partners in the Americas, the US appears to respond to the creation of market power, with an attempt to create more market power itself. This is a rational response if the US expects a united Europe to impose tariffs on the rest of the world. As discussed above, the emergence of a region with increased market power generally provides an incentive to other regions to seek similar status.

More explanatory power still can be extracted from the results of Kennan and Riezman [15, 16] and Riezman [25] on who wins trade wars. Following the creation of a custom union, the incentives are not just to create or join another free trade zone. The economic incentive is to join another free trade zone with the largest possible market power. This result allows us to predict that the US will seek a free trade deal with as many countries in the Americas as possible. The aim is to reach market power which exceeds that of a unified Europe.

The final result on world trade will however depend on the trade patterns adopted within the blocks. Trade patterns within the EU and NAFTA can be based either on traditional comparative advantages or on economies of scale. These are two different patterns of development, which can be broadly illustrated by Asian-type development strategies, which focus on knowlege-intensive products such as consumer electronics, communications and financial markets, and African and Latinamerican-style type development strategies, which focus instead on resources

---

[7] Lerner and Metzler do not refer to economies of scale: their results on the impact of tariffs on terms of trade are due to income effects.

and labor intensive products. The former emphasize products which rely on an educated labor force and human capital. The latter emphasizes resources and cheap, mostly uneducated, labor intensive products. It is to a certain extent a matter of policy choice which pattern of development is adopted. The choice is either products and technologies which are associated to *external* economies of scale, or those associated to traditional comparative advantages. In sum: trade policies within a trade block determine the extent to which the trade block will aid or hinder global free trade. The argument for this result, and its implications for trade policy, will occupy the rest of this paper.

3 Trade Creation and Diversion

3.1 The Traditional Case

How do we measure the gains and the losses of creating a free trade zone?

A naive view on this is that since free trade in competitive markets is Pareto efficient, any move towards free trade is positive. As we saw, this argument is not correct. Regional trade blocks, being larger than their components, will have more market power and therefore under traditional conditions will impose tariffs against outsiders. Therefore trading blocks hurt the countries outside these areas.

Are free trade zones only damaging to outsiders? The answer to this question is: generally no. There is a second source of potential damage. The trading block can lead to *trade diversion.* This means that a trade block may lead to the wrong specialization within the block. The classical argument about trade diversion is found in Viner [26], whose work remains a benchmark of analysis for preferential trade agreements. I summarize his argument here in order to show that, if trading within the blocks is organized around economies of scale, then Viner's argument can break down. With economies of scale, the negative effect of trade diversion can be mitigated. The empirical evidence discussed below suggests that this is what has happened in the European Common Market since 1958.

Viner's argument can be captured from the textbook table presented below:

There are three countries, Germany, Portugal and the USA. They trade a commodity, vegetable oil. Initially Germany has a tariff that applies equally to all imported oil, no matter what its source. If it imports oil despite the tariff, it will buy initially from the USA, which offers the best price. The example appears in the second column, showing a low initial tariff. However if the tariff is high enough, then Germany will produce its own oil, as in column 3. What happens if now Germany enters into a free trade agreement with Portugal?

If the tariff was initially the level indicated in column 2 of Figure 1, the welfare of Germany increases after the regional block is created, since it replaces its domestic oil with a less expensive oil and uses its domestic resources in

Cost of Veg. Oil	Tariffs		
	0	8	12
Germany	20	20	20
Portugal before EEC	16	24	28
Portugal after EEC	16	16	16
USA	10	18	22

Fig. 1. The effects of Trading Blocks: Trade Diversion.

more productive sectors. However, if the tariff was initially higher, as in column 3 of Figure 1, then after the free trade agreement Germany shifts from American to Portuguese oil, i.e. from a low cost to a higher cost producer. In this case, the free trade zone lowers welfare in the participating region. It has diverted trade.

Viner's point is that there are "trade creating" free trade zones, which increase imports by members from one another. These imports replace less efficient domestic production, and are therefore desirable. On the other hand, free trade blocks can "divert trade": imports can be diverted from a lower cost source outside the block to a less efficient source inside the block. The insider source could be less productive but may offer more attractive prices after the tariffs were selectively dropped. The latter trading is undesirable.

Extra trade among the members of the trading block can improve welfare. The trade which is a diversion from efficient outsiders to less efficient insiders, lowers welfare. For example if northern Europe is induced by the entry of southern Europe to buy oil from Portugal rather than an equivalent from the US, and the US source is more efficient but less competitive after the tariffs are dropped, there has been a welfare loss. Generally speaking Viner's approach evaluates free trade zones by the extent to which more trade is created, rather than existing trade diverted from one source to another.

3.2 Economies of Scale Mitigate Trade Diversion

Viner's original insight remains central to the analysis of preferential free trade zones. But, in practice, it misses an important aspect. The increased size of the market can sometimes lead to more efficiency and competitiveness. Even in the cases where Viner's analysis predicts welfare losses, namely when the trade block diverts trade to inside sources which are initially less competitive, welfare can still increase with economies of scale. This can be explained simply in our numerical example.

Cost of Veg. Oil	Tariffs		
	0	8	12
Germany	20	20	20
Portugal before EEC	16	24	28
Portugal after EEC	9	9	9
USA	10	18	22

Fig. 2. Trade is not Diverted with Economies of Scale.

As Portugal expands its oil production due to its new trade with Germany, it can become more efficient due to economies of scale. This situation is illustrated in Figure 2, column 1. After the tariffs are removed Portugal produces and exports more oil and in the process it becomes more competitive and its costs drop, reaching or improving upon the US level. In sum: with economies of scale, Viner's analysis is reversed.

Economies of scale can have a major impact on trade policies. They can check the negative effects of trade diversion. I shall argue in what follows that they can also limit another negative effect: the incentives for large blocks with market power to impose tariffs on outsiders. These are the two major drawbacks of trading blocks: tariff wars and trade diversion. Both drawbacks are reduced and could be eliminated in trade regimes based on economies of scale.

3.3 Empirical Evidence for Economies of Scale: Knowledge-intensive Growth

What does the empirical evidence show?[8] It is widely believed that economies of scale were an important factor in the Treaty of Rome. Economies of scale were central to the success of the European Common Market which was formed in 1958. While a strong possibility for trade diversion existed *a priori* in the EU, in reality

---

[8] Although the central body of international trade theory is based on the assumption of constant returns to scale, the belief is widespread that increasing returns are important in reality, and there is a large body of literature specifically addressing the issues that emerge. Classical references are Graham [12] and Viner [27]; modern references include Mathews [19] Meade [20] and more recently Chichilnisky and Heal [9] Chapter 3, Ethier [11], and Krugman and Obstfeld [17]. However the literature has neglected the issue of trading blocks with economies of scale as studied here. In fact, while the results of Graham and Viner argue that increasing returns to scale are a motive for protection, my results argue that, to the contrary, increasing returns provide a reason against tariffs, and for free trade.

huge inter-industry trade emerged in manufactures. The increase in market size and the associated rationalization in production led to efficiency gains which took precedence over possible trade diversion.

A discussion of the empirical evidence for economies of scale in the US and in Europe is in Chichilnisky and Heal [9], and the reader is referred to that source. Of particular interest are all sectors which require large scale production for efficiency such as automobile industry and aerospace. These were traditonally the most important sectors in the US economy. More recently, economies of scale became prominent in sectors where knowledge is an important input, such as computer processing, hardware and software, telecommunications, financial markets and genetic engineering. Chichilnisky and Heal [9] developed a rigorous foundations of international trade with increasing returns in a neoclassical model of trade with two countries and two goods, and discussed the policy implications of economies of scale for North-South trade.[9]

An interesting discussion on the matter of returns to scale is also in a recent paper which does not draw the connection between economies of scale, optimal tariffs and trade diversion, but provides evidence for the US-Canada case and for the EU[10]: "Indeed, hopes for large benefits from both the US-Canada free trade agreement and Europe 1992 rest largely on an increase in competition and rationalization. In the North American case, the estimate of Harris and Cox, which attempt to take account of competitive/industrial organization effects, suggest a gain for Canada from free trade that is about 4 time larger than those of standard models. In Europe the widely cited and somewhat controversial figure of 7 percent gain due to 1992 presented in the Cechini report of the Commission of the European Communities 1988 rests primarily on estimates by Alisdair Smith and Anthony Venables of gains from increased competition and rationalization."

A standard textbook analysis of economies of scale is in Nicholson [24], "Costs", pages 252–255, who documents that most studies of long-run cost curves have found that average costs are decreasing up to a point and then constant. Examples provided are agriculture, electricity generation, railroads, and commercial banking, all activites which are broadly associated with economic development. The same textbook analysis explains how competitive markets can lead to a negative association of quantities and prices across equilibria which is typical of economies of scale. This was the content of the famous debate in the 1920's between J. H. Clapham, A. C. Pigou and D. H. Robertson, which was resolved positively, and which appeared in the Economic Journal between 1922 and 1924,

---

[9] They show that when the North exports goods with economies of scale and the South exports goods without, the North benefits from trade expansion, but the South's term of trade typically drop, Chapter 3.

[10] See P. Krugman "The Move to Free Trade Zones" Working Paper, Economics Department, MIT, 1991, presented at the UN-ECLA June 1992 Conference on Trade Liberalization in the Americas, Washington D.C.

see Nicholson [24], "Perfectly Competitive Pricing in the Long Run" page 332. These authors agree that competitive markets *can* show a negative association between prices and quantities in the long run. A typical example of this phenomenon is the computer industry. Chichilnisky and Heal [9] have discussed in some detail the policy implications of international trade in economies with increasing returns to scale in a report on trade policies in the 1980's to the Secretary General of UNCTAD. They arrive at similar conclusions.

I have argued that economies of scale can defeat trade diversion, and transform the attendant potential losses into gains. I will also argue below that increasing returns can defeat the incentives for tariff wars between blocks. Trade diversion and tariffs are the main forces which oppose the simultaneous development of trading blocks and free world trade. Therefore the formation of trading blocks with increasing returns can become a parallel, complementary effort towards the liberalization of world trade.

4 Trading Blocks With Economies of Scale

4.1 Trade Inside and Between the Blocks

Although predictions are inherently dangerous in an area so circumscribed by political action, my conclusion is that trade blocks can have different effects on global markets depending on their structure. It is the choice of well informed and reasonable economic agents which structure will prevail.

Regional trading blocks based on traditional comparative advantages will generally divert trade. They will also typically hinder the propects of global negotiations. In this case, as the block has more market power then its parts, it has the incentive to impose tariffs on the rest of the world. Regional blocks develop incentives for trade wars. This type of regional free trade zone works against global free trade.

However, if trade blocks are oriented to the expansion of trade based on increased size and on the productive efficiency and competitiveness that comes with economies of scale, matters are different. In this latter case, the regional free trade zones could unleash an appetite for further expansion of trade. In this case the incentive for blocks to impose tariffs is reduced, and can be defeated by the incentive in favor of trade expansion which accompanies economies of scale. The incentives are now for further expansion of trade. The creation of trading blocks which are organized around economies of scale is therefore part of a broader trend towards increasingly open world markets.

5 The Americas: Traditional Comparative Advantage or Economies of Scale

The pattern of trade inside the blocks is of particular importance for an American free trade zone. Trade within NAFTA is mosty based on traditional comparative advantage and on the diversity between the traders' economic development rather than on economies of scale. Exports from Mexico to the US are mostly petroleum or resource based products, a pattern which holds also for the rest of Latin America. Therefore NAFTA's characteristics are unfavourable to global free trade.

The matter is not only one of economic reality: it is also one of perceived economic reality. Both the European and the East Asian countries perceive gains from trade as a matter of exploiting economies of scale. The newly industrialized countries in Asia, and the Japanese, have a dynamic vision of comparative advantages. Moving up the ladder of comparative advantages in the production and trade of skilled-labor manufactures, of consumer electronics, and of products based on specialized knowledge and on technological skill, are widespread priorities.

By contrast, within the sphere of influence of the US, the vision of trade based on traditional comparative advantages still prevails. It permeates to a great extent the thinking about international trade at the government level, at the international organization level, at the academic, and even at the journalistic level.

The European free trade zone is, to a certain extent, a zone of equals. To encourage this equality, the free mobility of labor has been one of the first steps in the European integration of 1992.

The Americas, on the other hand, have the US as a hegemon, a "hub" which concentrates on exporting manufactures and skill intensive goods to the "spokes" in exchange for their resources. The free mobility of labor between the hub and the spokes is an unspoken issue. It has not even been contemplated in the American negotiations for free trade. It has not been mentioned by any of the governments concerned that labor could move freely between the NAFTA trade partners, as it is in the EU. In some cases, quite to the contrary, the free trade agreement has been mentioned as a way to limit the mobility of labor between the concerned countries, such as Mexico and the US.

To the extent that labor remains a fixed input of production within the countries of the Americas, traditional comparative advantages based on labor will be invoked as a foundation for policy. The concern is that an American free trade zone, if it emerges, may reflect the historical patterns of trade between industrial and developing regions, which is usually called North-South trade. These patterns would not be conducive to the overall liberalization of world trade.

6 Traditional Comparative Advantage and the Global Environment

The global environment provides another argument against traditional comparative advantages. Traditional comparative advantages emphasize the South's concentration in the production and export of goods which deplete environmental resources, such as wood pulp and cash crops which overuse rain forests, and fossil fuels and minerals whose combustion leads to the emission of greenhouse gases. Recent work in the area of North-South trade with environmental inputs to production (Chichilnisky [6, 7]) shows that poorly defined patterns of property rights on forests, fisheries, and arable land in developing countries may lead to a market-induced oversupply of products which are intensive in the use of these resources, and to Pareto inefficient patterns of international trade. Indeed, it is shown in Chichilnisky [6, 7] that differences in property rights can by themselves explain the patterns of trade between nations. What appears as comparative advantages may simply be a reflection of a market failure which through the magnifying glass of international trade leads to an inefficient overuse of resources in the entire world economy. Social and private comparative advantages differ, and social and private gains from trade may also differ in these circumstances [6, 7].

The global environment is therefore another argument against traditional comparative advantages as a foundation for trade.[11] Since two thirds of the current exports from Latin America are resources, and the main trade of Ecuador, Venezuela and Mexico with the US is petroleum, this problem is very real. It is also very real with respect to the trading in wood products which lead to the deforestations of the remaining tropical forests in Central and South America [1–3, 13]. Petroleum extraction in Ecuador destroys its Amazonian resources. Replacing traditional comparative advantages with economies of scale could be a necessary feature of a program of sustainable development.

7 External Economies of Scale are Labor and Knowledge Intensive

It seems desirable at this point to distinguish between two types of economies of scale: internal to the firm, or external to it. The former occur when each firm is more efficient in the use of its inputs to production as the level of its output increases. Such economies of scale are typical of traditional industries which require large fixed costs, such as aerospace, airlines, and automobiles. This type of increasing returns, called internal, can lead to monopolistic competition or other

---

[11] Tradional tax policies, levying duties on the use of such inputs in the South, may not work if they lead to lower income levels, and may indeed lead to more extraction of the resource and more exports of the resource intensive commodity. Property rights policies may be more effective in this case.

forms of limitations to market entry. There is a loss to the consumer because free market outcomes are typically not Pareto efficient when firms have market power and can influence prices.

There is a different type: external economies of scale. These also lead to a decrease in per unit costs as the ouput expands, but they do so at the level of the industry or of the country as a whole. Each firm's production function faces increasing cost per unit of output, i.e. decreasing returns to scale, which assures competitive behavior. However, as the industry expands, externalities are created which lead to increased productivity for all the firms. A good example is provided by the electronics industry. Each computer manufacturer faces a competitive market. On the other hand, as the overall level of output of the industry expands, knowledge about new technologies develops and is rapidly diffused across the industry leading to lower costs for all. Any industry which depends heavily on knowledge has this characteristic. Increasing returns originate in the skill of labor, which embodies knowledge. Knowledge is typically diffused and can be captured and imitated sooner or later. There are abundant examples in the software and hardware industry to prove this point[12]. Knowledge creates skilled labor, and this in turn leads to increasing returns to scale, which are often external to the firm. This can lead simultaneously to economies of scale and to competitive markets. The successful development experiences of Japan, Korea, Taiwan, and more generally the Asian Tigers, shows that export-led policies based on skilled labor intensive goods, for example in consumer electronics, is more successful than those based on inexpensive and uneducated labor. This point was developed formally in Chichilnisky [5], [4], and more recently of Dadzie [10].

In this paper I concentrate on external economies of scale, which are closely connected with production system based on skilled labor. It should be noted that the areas most favorable to external economies of scale, such as software production, are labor intensive rather than capital intensive. Therefore they are particularly well suited for developing countries with abundant and skilled labor.[13]

8 Optimal Tariffs

8.1 Traditional Theory With Decreasing Returns

A second traditional concern about trade blocks is that they generate incentives to levy tariffs on outsiders. I mentioned above that, under traditional assumptions, a large country will typically impose tariffs so as to improve its terms of

---

[12] Microsoft's Windows excellent imitation of the Apple operating system was tested in the US courts and found without fault.

[13] India is a good example; it exports software news succesfully. So is Mexico, which produces chips. Barbados is planning a shift to an information-age society in one generation.

trade. In doing so it typically introduces distortions in its production and consumption. Here I will show in a simple example how under traditional assumptions there is a tariff that improves welfare, in the sense that the gains from improved terms of trade exceed the losses from distortions. The analysis is completely standard, but it is included in order to highlight the differences which arise in economies with increasing returns to scale. This section discusses economies with decreasing returns: the next section discusses economies with increasing returns.

The analysis in this section relies on one assumption and one simplification. Both are lifted in the Appendix, which considers the general case. The assumption here is that the supply and demand curves of the economy are linear and, as already mentioned, supply exhibits decreasing returns to scale.[14] The simplification is to neglect the impact of the tariff revenues on income; this is typically done in textbooks, and will also be done in this section. It is however explicitly analyzed in the Appendix.

Assume that the home country H has a demand curve with equation

$$D = a - b\tilde{p}, \tag{1}$$

where $\tilde{p}$ is the domestic price of the good, and a supply curve

$$Q = e + f\tilde{p}. \tag{2}$$

Contry H's demand for imports is the difference

$$D - Q = (a - e) - (b + f)\tilde{p}. \tag{3}$$

Foreign export supply is also a straight line

$$(Q^* - D^*) = g + hp_w, \tag{4}$$

where p_w is the world price. The internal price in country H exceeds the world price by the tariff:

$$\tilde{p} = p_w + t. \tag{5}$$

In a world equilibrium imports must equal exports:

$$(a - e) - (b + f)(p_w + t) = g + hp_w. \tag{6}$$

---

[14] See e.g. [17], Appendix to Chapter 9.

Solving equation (6) for $t=0$ gives p_f, the world price that would prevail without tariffs. Then a tariff t alters the internal price to:

$$\tilde{p} = p_f + th/(b + f + h),\tag{7}$$

and the world price to

$$p_w = p_f - t(b + f)/(b + f + h).\tag{8}$$

Note that if the parameters a, e, b, h and f are all positive, then

$$p_f < \tilde{p} \quad \text{and} \quad p_w < p_f,\tag{9}$$

implying that *the tariff raises the internal price $\tilde{p}$ and lowers the world price p_w.*

It is immediate to show that, under these conditions, it is always possible to find a tariff t that increases the country's welfare. Let q_1 and d_1 be the free trade levels of consumption and production. Since the internal prive is higher after the tariff, domestic supply rises from q_1 to q_2 and demand falls from d_1 to d_2:

$$q_2 = q_1 + tfh/(b + f + h)\tag{10}$$

and

$$d_2 = d_1 - tbh/(b + f + h).\tag{11}$$

The gain in welfare from a lower world price is the area of the rectangle in Figure 3, the fall in the price multiplied by the level of imports after the tariff:

$$\text{gain in welfare} = (d_2 - q_2) \times t(b + f)/(b + f + h)$$
$$= t \times (d_1 - q_1) \times (b + f)/(b + f + h) - (t)^2 \times h(b + f)^2/(b + f + h)^2.\tag{12}$$

The loss from distorted consumption is the sum of the areas of the two triangles in Figure 3:

$$\text{loss in welfare} = (1/2) \times (q_2 - q_1) \times (\tilde{p} - p_f) + (1/2) \times (d_1 - d_2) \times (\tilde{p} - p_f)$$
$$= (t)^2 \times (b + f) \times h^2/2(b + f + h)^2.\tag{13}$$

Therefore the net effect on welfare is

$$\text{gain} - \text{loss} = t \times U - (t)^2 \times V.\tag{14}$$

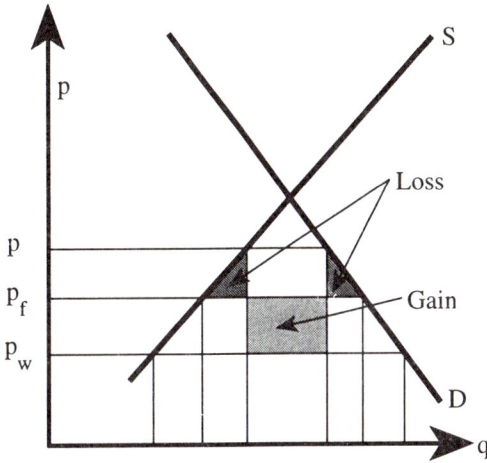

Fig. 3. Gains and Losses from Tariffs: Traditional Case.

where U and V are constants. The net effect is the sum of a positive number times the tariff rate and a negative number times the square of the tariff rate. It follows that when the tariff is sufficiently small the net effect must be positive, since t^2 is smaller than t, for t near zero. This establishes that, when supply and demand are linear, income effects of the tariff income are neglected and tariffs are small, there exists a positive tariff which increases the welfare of the country beyond that which can be obtained in free trade. Therefore there is a positive *optimal tariff.*

Of course, the size of the country matters. If the importing country is small, then foreign supply is highly elastic i.e. h is very large, so from (8) one verifies that the tariff has little or no effect on world prices p_w while raising domestic prices $\tilde{p}$ almost one-to-one.

8.2 Optimal Tariffs With Economies of Scale

The argument in the previous section shows that under traditional assumptions a large country is better off by imposing tariffs than it is under free trade. This proposition holds when the supply of goods increases with prices. In our example, this is formalized by the parameters in the supply function in equation (2), which is upward sloping. However, this assumption ceases to be valid when the economy has economies of scale. In such economies the larger is the output the lower are the costs, and therefore, in principle, the lower are the prices. Then $f < 0$ in equation (8) or $h < 0$ in equation (4) which in turn can lead to a negative welfare gain from the tariff from equation (12).

A good example of this phenomenon is provided by the electronics industry, for example, computer hardware. The last fifteen years have seen a dramatic decrease in prices together with a dramatic expansion of output of computer hardware. This occurs because the expansion in output leads to rationalization and the corresponding increased efficiency in production. In the hardware industry this takes the form of technological change which improves productive efficiency and lowers the costs of the industry as a whole. Even though a technological breakthrough may in principle be patented, and therefore could be captured by one firm with the corresponding increase in its market power and deviation from competitive behavior, in practice the computer industry is very competitive. This is because the knowledge which drives the technological innovation in this industry is easily diffused.

I shall now show how the analysis of optimal tariffs in the last section breaks down when there are increasing returns to scale. In such economies there may be no gains from imposing tariffs, even if the country is large and has substantial market power. The optimal tariff theorem no longer holds. I will explain how this happens in a concrete case.

It is useful to recall first how tariffs increase welfare in the economy of the previous section. Tariffs increase welfare by lowering the world prices p_w: this was seen in equation (7). The country's terms of trade thus improve after the tariff: It imports fewer lower cost goods from the rest of the world. The welfare gains were computed in equation (12): these depend crucially on the fact that, after the tariff, the consumers pay lower prices for the goods they import.

However, this argument no longer hold with economies of scale. With economies of scale the world price may *increase* rather than decrease after the tariff. The welfare gains from tariffs are measured by the drop in world prices times the quantity imported. But if the world price increases, the gains become losses.

After a tariff the terms of trade can deteriorate for the country; this was studied in A. Lerner [18] and in L. Metzler [23]. They argue mostly in terms of income effects, not in terms of increasing returns. A similar phenomenon occurs in economies with increasing returns, but due to different causes. With increasing returns, in constrast with the economy of the previous section, the parameters f and h in equations (8) and (4) are negative rather than positive. This means that across equilibria the prices drop as quantities increase, or otherwise, price increase when quantities drop. If the tariff decreases the quantitiy produced and traded, this lowers the efficiency of the economy. Costs increase and therefore prices increase too. The tariff defeats the gains from rationalization in production produced by the larger market size. This is represented in Figure 4 above. It shows a negative correlation between market clearing prices and the quantity of goods sold at an equilibrium, and how this can lead to an increase in the world prices after the tariff, corresponding with the decrease in output.

With increasing returns, after the tariff, the world price p_w can be higher with rather than lower as it is in the traditional case.[15] The terms of trade for the country

---

[15] A formal proof is in the Appendix.

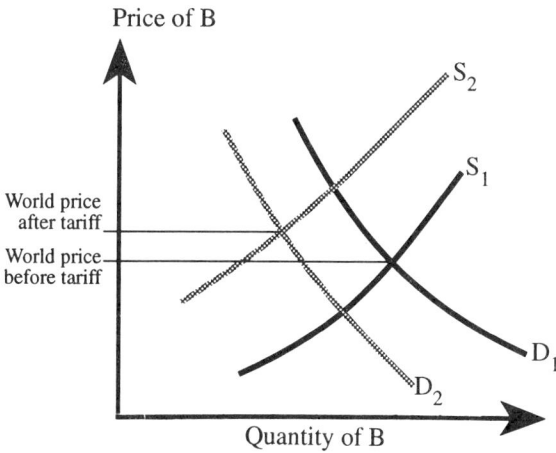

Fig. 4. Losses from Tariffs with Increasing Returns. International Market equilibrium: S_1 and D_1 are the supply and demand for exports and imports of B, respectively, at the first equilibrium without tariffs. The tariff shifts downward the demand schedule to D_2. The lower quantity exported (x) is associated to less efficiency and therefore to higher prices, due to increasing returns to scale. For a mathematical analysis, see the Appendix.

are therefore worse after the tariff. Consumers in the country are worse off: the price of their imports have increased. All of this is established rigorously in the appendix.

A economies of scale, the optimal tariff theorem is no longer true. The region's terms of trade can decrease with the imposition of tariffs, so that the importing region has no incentive to impose tariffs on others: it looses by restricting trade.

Consumer electronics, semiconductors, software production, banking and financial services, and any sector whose productivity depends mostly on knowledge and information have these characteristics. Software production is today actively developed in India as an export business. It is a sector which is simultaneously labor and knowledge intensive and subject to economies of scale. As already discussed the remarkable economic development of the Asian Tigers over the last fifteen years profited from the expansion of their international trade of skilled-labor intensive products such as consumer electronics. This sector is simultaneously labor intensive and subject to economies of scale.

All the arguments just presented hold equally for countries or for trading blocks. To the extent that sectors with economies of scale expand within the free trade zone, the zone itself loses its economic incentives to use its market power to restrict trade and to wage tariff wars.

9 Conclusions

I have argued that the formation of trading blocks harms the liberalization of markets when the blocks are organized around traditional comparative advantages. Under these conditions, the larger is the market power of the block, the larger are its incentives to impose tariffs. Protectionism emerges from the increased market power of the traders.

Retaliation can lead to a tariff war between the blocks. Furthermore under traditional assumptions, the larger country wins the tariff war. Therefore the larger is the trading block, the more likely it is to impose tariffs and to win a trade war.

Trading blocks of this nature have no economic incentive to favor world's free trade. They are better of with tariffs than with free trade. I argued that, to a certain extent, this explains the difficulties of the Gatt negotiations.

I discussed the example of the EU block in contrast with NAFTA. The evidence suggests that the EU benefited from increasing returns to scale.

NAFTA, and any eventual America free trading block, emerged as a strategic response to the increased market power of the European trading block. By contrast with the EU, the emerging NAFTA appears to be organizing under the traditional theory of comparative advantage.

The lack of any provision for the mobility of labor between the countries of the region reinforces this trend. NAFTA does not contemplate the mobility of labor between Mexico and the US. The lack of labor mobility tends to lock-in the traditonal comparative advantages between the countries within the area. Their trading of the basis of comparative advantages *within* the block will create incentives for trade wars *between* the blocks.

But NAFTA could be organized around economies of scale. Examples for such scenarios include Indian software trade, and the Asian Tigers' specialization in consumer electronics. Typically, electronic-based industries have increasing returns derived from the creation and diffusion of knowledge as output expands. This leads to rationalization in production and to increased efficiency and thus lower costs. The expansion of output is accompanied by lower rather than higher prices. From the point of view of the exporter, these markets are less likely to be protected because the importer, having increasing returns to scale in this industry, has less incentives to rely on tariffs than it does in other industries with decreasing returns. With increasing returns, tariffs decrease trade and can increase world prices, thus decreasing the welfare of the importing country. Economies of scale produce incentives to expand trade.

Economies of scale can defeat the standard result on optimal tariffs. While under traditional conditions, a trading block is always better of with tariffs than it is with free trade, with increasing returns to scale this is no longer true. Tariffs decrease the size of the market, and therefore decrease productive efficiency in economies with increasing returns. This decrease in efficiency leads to larger rather than lower world prices, and the main purpose of the tariff, which is to improve the countries' terms of trade defeat. Under these conditions trading blocks are better of with free trade and with the corresponding expanded market, than they are with tariffs.

To the extent that NAFTA organizes itself around economies of scale the incentives for a trade wars between NAFTA and the EC are mitigated.

It seems useful to remind ourselves that the choice of products and of technology are, to a certain extent, open to policy. Countries with good educational systems, developed or not, can choose to follow development patterns with a concentration of knowledge-intensive products, avoiding the over exploitation of natural resources and exports of uneducated labor-intensive products. Those countries with poor educational systems can do better by investing in human capital and thus opening knowlege-intensive patterns of development for their future.

In any case, a choice of product, need not interfere with market efficiency. The first welfare theorem about the efficiency of competitive markets applies to a market with given technologies and with given products. The theorem does not explain how different technologies or products arise: it proves that once technologies and products are given, competive markets lead to Pareto efficiency. Once the product mix and the technologies are chosen the market can operate efficiently. This implies that the organizing principles within the blocks – traditional comparative advantages or economies of scale – are, to a certain extent, a policy choice. Technologies and a different product mix can be achieved without market distortions or loss of market efficiency. This point was already made by James Meade several years ago [22].

The emergence of an American trading block which reinforces the current tendency toward the exploitation of traditonal comparative advantages is a source of concern. It has been argued Chichilnisky [4, 5, 9] that export led policies based on (unskilled) labor intensive products can defeat the goals of development and trade by depressing the country's terms of trade and overall consumption. Trade between the countries of the Americas is organized today around traditonal comparative advantages: labor and resource intensive exports from the South and capital and skill-intensive exports from the North. If the emergence of an America free trade zone is based on similar principles, then not only may this continue a depressing growth trend in Latin America, but in addition it could create or reinforce incentives against the global liberalization of free trade.

Another reason to avoid trade policies based on traditional comparative advantages is that they tend to deplete environmental assets such as forests, fisheries or fertile land, and overuse minerals which are exported by the developing countries to the North. Some of these minerals are the source of potentially dangerous CO_2 emissions. Petroleum exported from Mexico, Ecuador and Venezuela to the USA fits this description. Indeed, any concept of *sustainable development* requires a rethinking of trade policies away from those based on comparative advantages. This general premise is particularly well suited to the NAFTA, and to the Americas as a whole, since two thirds of Latin American exports today are resources.

The main point of this paper is that the characteristics of trading policies *within* the trading blocks can determine the extent to which the block will favor or harm global free trade. Trading policies based on comparative advantages are generally negative. Trading policies based on economies of scale can be positive. They can mitigate the economic incentive towards tariffs and favor instead the expansion of world's trade. The emergence of such trading blocks could advance in tandem with the global liberalization of trade.

10 Appendix: Trading Blocks with Endogenous Technology and Increasing Returns to Scale

10.1 A Two Region Two Good Model With Endogenous Technology and Economies of Scale

This appendix introduces and develops an international trade model, and proves rigorously the propositions stated in the body of the paper.

The model presented here extends the North-South model introduced in Chichilnisky [4, 5, 9] in several directions. One is to allow technologies given by Cobb-Douglas production functions;[16] a second aspect is that countries here trade in goods produced under conditions of increasing returns to scale, while previous work considered constant returns to scale.

At least one of the goods (B) is produced here under increasing returns to scale; the second good (I) could be produced either with constant returns or with increasing returns to scale. A novel aspect of this model is that the increasing returns are here *external* to the firm: each firm takes technology as given, a Cobb-Douglas production function with constant returns, multiplied by a coefficient γ. This parameter γ is treated as given by the firm. However γ varies with the production of the whole sector, making all those firms having increasing returns simultaneously more productive at an equilibrium in which more is produced. Therefore technologies are *endogenous:* the returns to scale of each sector are endogenously determined along with all other variables, at the equilibrium. Competitive markets are assumed throughout: firms maximize profits and the classic marginal conditions prevail.

The material is presented as follows: first I formulate the model for one region; then I extend this to two trading regions. I then find one explicit equation, a

---

[16] Chichilnisky [4, 5] considered fixed coefficients technologies.

"resolving equation", which solves the model analytically as a function of only one variable: the terms of trade. From this equation one calculates analytically a complete solution of the model from the values of its exogenous parameters, by solving for the equilibrium values of the terms of trade. Finally I establish formally that, with increasing returns to scale, large countries can achieve higher welfare levels with free trade than with tariffs. This means that increasing returns can defeat the optimal tariff theorem.

The model describes two regions, 1 and 2, producing and trading two goods B (basic goods) and I (industrial goods) with each other; these goods are produced using two inputs, labor L and capital, K. The economies of the two countries are competitive, so that in each region prices are taken as given by consumers and producers. Producers maximize profits, and consumers maximize utility subject to their budget constraints. Walras Law is satisfied, so that the value of the excess demand is equal to zero. At an equilibrium all markets, for goods and for factors, clear.

The *increasing returns to scale* considered here are "external" to the firm as in the examples discussed in the text. This means that in the production functions, formalized below, the parameter γ increases with the total level of output of the economy. As the output of the economy expands, the production function varies, formalizing the notion that factors are more productive at higher levels of aggregate output. To obtain the results presented here, all that is required is that the production function becomes more productive as the output of *one* of the good (B) increases. The firms take this parameters γ as given – this is the assumption that the increasing returns are external to the firm. For each given value of the parameter γ the firm has constant returns to scale. The firms are therefore competitive, and in particular zero profits are achieved at an equilibrium.

10.2 One Region Model

Consider the model of one region first. The production fuctions are[17]

$$B^s = \gamma L_1^\alpha K_1^{1-\alpha}$$
$$I^s = \gamma L_2^\beta K_2^{1-\beta} \tag{16}$$

---

[17] Note that there is no specification of supply behaviour outside of equilibrium, because as far as the firm is concerned there are constant returns to scale in production so that profit maximizing supply functions are, as is standard with constant returns, undefined. As is standard, one derives supply and demand simultaneously at an equilibrium from the condition of full employment of factors and market clearing, and in this model this is done together with a condition which incorporates the simultaneous determination of the parameter giving the extent of economies of scale.

where $\alpha, \beta \in (0,1)$, γ is a positive parameter determining returns to scale which is determined endogenously at an equilibrium, L_1 and K_1 are the inputs of labor and capital in the B sector, and L_2 and K_2 the inputs of labor and capital in the I sector. The total amount of labor and capital in the economy are L^s and K^s respectively. Prices are p_B and p_I; we assume that I is the numeraire so that

$$p_I = 1. \tag{17}$$

Factor prices are denoted as usual: w for wages and r for rental on capital. I shall assume for simplicity that the demand for basic goods at an equilibrium is known:

$$B^d = \mu(wL) + (1 - \mu)rK, \quad 0 \le \mu \le 1. \tag{18}$$

By Walras Law the demand for industrial goods in equilibrium is

$$I^d = (wL^s + rK^s - p_B B^d), \tag{19}$$

because there are zero profits derived from the firm's profit maximization under constant returns to scale. Demand functions other than (18) can be postulated without changing the results, see for example the various demand functions utilized in Chichilnisky [5]. Indicating the equilibrium level of exports by X_B^{s*} and the equilibrium level of imports by X_I^{d*}, the model of the world economy is formalized by the following equilibrium conditions:

$$p_B^* B^{s*} + I^* = w^* L^* + r^* K^* \quad \text{(zero profits)}$$

$$K^* = K^s = K_1 + K_2 \quad \text{(capital market clears)}$$

$$L^* = L^s = L_1 + L_2 \quad \text{(labor market clears)} \tag{20}$$

$$B^{s*} = B^{d*} + X_B^{s*} \quad \text{(B market clears)}$$

$$I^{d*} = I^{s*} + X_I^{d*} \quad \text{(I market clears)}$$

$$\gamma = \gamma(B^*, I^*) \quad \text{(endogenous technology)}.$$

10.3 Two Region Model

The model for the world economy consists of two regions, indicated with the indices 1 and 2, each specified as above. To solve the model, there are therefore five prices to the determined: the "terms of trade" p_B, and two factor prices in each country: w an r. The quantities to be determined in an equilibrium are the use of factors in each sector of each region: K_1, K_2, L_1, L_2 and the outputs of the two goods B^s and I^s. At the equilibrium one obtains endogenously the value of the parameter γ determining the external economies of scale in each sector of the economy $\gamma = \gamma(B^*, I^*)$. At an equilibrium one also determines the exports and imports of each of the two goods in each of the two regions, X_B^{s*} and X_I^{d*}, and the demand for each good in each region: $B^{d*} I^{d*}$. There is therefore a total of *twenty seven* variables to be determined endogenously at an equilibrium, including all prices and quantities in all markets and in both regions.

The following Proposition 1 proves that all of these variables can be determined once the variable giving the terms of trade in equilibrium p_B is known. Furthermore I prove that there exists *one* "resolving equation" which determines the equilibrium value of the terms of trade as a function of all the exogenous parameters of the model.

The are *six* exogenous parameters in each region: $\alpha, \beta, \sigma, B^{d*}, L^s$ and K^s, and a total of *twelve* in the world economy. The impact of changes in each of these parameters on the equilibrium of the model can be traced analytically via the "resolving equation".

10.4 Solving the Model With a Single "Resolving" Equation in the Terms of Trade

Proposition 1

There exists one "resolving" equation depending only on the terms of trade, from which a complete solution of the two region model can be computed explicitly as a function of all the exogenous parameters of the model.

Proof

The proof consists of writing the market clearing conditions on the world market for B and substituting step by step until one finds one expression which depends on all the exogenous parameters of the model and only on one variable: the terms of trade. Then I show that all other endogenous variables can be found once the terms of trade are known, including of course the value of the returns to scale parameter γ which defines the technology. The proof proceeds in a number of steps. In step 1, I express the labor and capital ratios used in the two industries l_1 and l_2, as functions of the terms of trade, p_B. Step 2 express the level of capital and labor used a functions of p_B. Step 3 expresses output in the two sectors as functions of p_B and the technology parameter γ. Step 4 expresses the output levels in the two sectors as a function of p_B alone, by carrying out a simple "fixed point" argument on the technology parameter γ. Step 5 expresses the international market claring con-

dition in the B market as a function of p_B alone, thus producing the desired
"resolving equation". Finally, Step 6 shows how all endogenous variables in the
model are determined once p_B is known.

Consider a world economy with two regions defined as in equations (16–20). I
now solve the model by finding an explicit expression for the equilibrium terms of
trade p_B^* in the world economy. I shall use the indices 1 and 2 to distinguish the
parameters of the two countries. It is important to observe that since I have given
no specification of demand or supply behaviour outside of an equilibrium, there is
no information for carrying out stability analysis. Since the model has constant
returns to scale, profit maximizing supply functions are, as is standard, undefined.
In fact, there are many possible and equally good specifications of disequilibrium
behaviour in this model, each leading to different stability properties (which are
not analyzed here). For stability analysis, see Chichilnisky [4] and [5]. As is
standard in models with constant returns to scale, derive the equilibrium relations
between supplies and prices from the condition of full employment of factors
together with an equilibrium condition which incorporates the external economies
of scale.

Step 1: express the labor and capital ratios used in the two industries as a function
of the term of trade. The strategy is to used logarithmic expressions and then
convert these. Denote:

$$l_1 = L_1/K_1$$

$$l_2 = L_2/K_2$$

Since by assumption each firm takes the parameter γ as given, from the production
functions (16), marginal conditions and zero profits imply:

$$w = \gamma\alpha(L_1/K_1)^{\alpha-1}p_B = \gamma\alpha l_1^{\alpha-1}p_B$$

$$r = \gamma(1-\alpha)l_1^{\alpha}p_B \tag{21}$$

and

$$w = \gamma\beta l_2^{\beta-1}$$

$$r = \gamma(1-\beta)l_2^{\beta} \tag{22}$$

so that

$$\frac{r}{w} = \left[\frac{(1-\alpha)}{\alpha}\right]l_1 \quad \text{and} \quad \frac{r}{w} = \left[\frac{(1-\beta)}{\beta}\right]l_2 \tag{23}$$

and in particular

$$l_1 = \frac{[(1-\beta)\alpha]}{[\beta(1-\alpha)]} l_2. \tag{24}$$

Indicating natural logarithms with the symbol "~" the four equations in (21) and (22) can be rewritten as:

$$\tilde{w} = (\alpha - 1)\tilde{l}_1 + \tilde{\alpha} + \tilde{p}_B + \tilde{\gamma}$$

$$\tilde{r} = \alpha\tilde{l}_1 + (1\widetilde{}\alpha) + \tilde{p}_B + \tilde{\gamma}$$

$$\tilde{w} = (\beta - 1)\tilde{l}_2 + \tilde{\beta} + \tilde{\gamma}$$

$$\tilde{r} = \beta\tilde{l}_2 + (1 - \beta) + \tilde{\gamma}. \tag{25}$$

so that

$$(\alpha - 1)\tilde{l}_1 + \tilde{\alpha} + \tilde{p}_B = (\beta - 1)\tilde{l}_2 + \tilde{\beta} \tag{26}$$

and

$$\alpha\tilde{l}_1 + (1\widetilde{}\alpha) + \tilde{p}_B = \beta\tilde{l}_2 + (1\widetilde{}\beta), \tag{27}$$

or equivalently

$$(\alpha - 1)\tilde{l}_1 + (1 - \beta)\tilde{l}_2 = \tilde{\beta} - \tilde{p}_B - \tilde{\alpha}$$

$$\alpha\tilde{l}_1 - \beta\tilde{l}_2 = (1\widetilde{}\beta) - \tilde{p}_B - (1\widetilde{}\alpha). \tag{28}$$

Solving the system (28) of two linear equations in $\tilde{l}_1, \tilde{l}_2$ one obtains:

$$\tilde{l}_1 = \frac{[(\tilde{\beta} - \tilde{p}_B - \tilde{\alpha})(-\beta) - (1-\beta)[(1\widetilde{}\beta) - \tilde{p}_B - (1\widetilde{}\alpha)]}{[\beta - \alpha]} \tag{29}$$

and

$$\tilde{l}_2 = \frac{[(\alpha - 1)[(1\widetilde{}\beta) - \tilde{p}_B - (1\widetilde{}\alpha)] - [(\tilde{\beta} - \tilde{p}_B - \tilde{\alpha})\alpha]]}{[\beta - \alpha]} \tag{30}$$

From (29) and (30) one obtains:

$$\tilde{l}_1 = \frac{\tilde{p}_B}{(\beta - \alpha)} + A \tag{31}$$

and

$$\tilde{l}_2 = \frac{\tilde{p}_B}{(\beta - \alpha)} + B$$

where

$$A = \frac{[(\tilde{\beta} - \tilde{\alpha})(-\beta) - (1 - \beta)[(1 \widetilde{} \beta) - (1 \widetilde{} \alpha)]]}{(\beta - \alpha)}$$

and

$$B = \frac{[(\alpha - 1)[(1 \widetilde{} \beta) - (1 \widetilde{} \alpha)] - \alpha(\tilde{\beta} - \tilde{\alpha})}{(\beta - \alpha)},$$

with $A > 0$ and $B < 0$ if $\beta < \alpha$. Therefore

$$l_1 = e^A p_B^{1/(\beta - \alpha)} \tag{32}$$

and

$$l_2 = e^B p_B^{1/(\beta - \alpha)}.$$

Step 1 is therefore completed: l_1 and l_2 are expressed as functions of terms of trade p_B.

Step 2: Express labor and capital used as function of p_B. Since

$$l_2 = \frac{(L^s - L_1)}{K^s - K_1} \Rightarrow L^s - L_1 = l_2(K^s - K_1) \text{ or } L_1 = L^s - l_2(K^s - K_1) \tag{33}$$

and

$$l_1 = L_1/K_1 \Rightarrow L_1 = l_1 K_1 \text{ so that by (33) } L^s - l_2(K^s - K_1) = l_1 K_1 \tag{34}$$

$$\Rightarrow K_1(l_1 - l_2) = L^s - l_2 K^s \text{ and } K_1 = (L^s - l_2 K^s)/(l_1 - l_2). \tag{35}$$

From (33)–(35) one obtains:

$$K_1 = \frac{(L^s - l_2 K^s)}{(l_1 - l_2)}$$ (36)

and

$$L_1 = \frac{(l_1)}{(l_1 - l_2)}(L^s - l_2 K^s)$$ (37)

from which together with (32) one obtains the levels of supply of labor and capital used in each sector at an equilibrium, as a function of the equilibrium level of the relative price of B:

$$L_1 = \frac{e^A L^s}{(e^A - e^B)} - \frac{e^A e^B}{(e^A - e^B)} K^s p_B^{1/(\beta - \alpha)}$$ (38)

and

$$K_1 = \frac{L^s}{e^A - e^B} p_B^{1/\alpha - \beta} - e^B(e^A - e^B) K^s$$ (39)

thus completing Step 2 of the proof. *Step 3* is to express output levels as a function of the terms of trade. From (16), (38) and (39) one obtains the quantity of B and I produced at each level of relative prices, p_B. Since these relations hold for every level of γ, taking $\gamma = 1$, I denote these as $\phi(p_B)$ and $\psi(p_B)$ respectively. Therefore from (16) one obtains the equilibrium level of outputs as a function of equilibrium prices:

$$B^s = \gamma\phi(p_B).$$ (40)

In the case that the sector I has also external economies of scale – which is not a necessary assumption for the results, one obtains similarly:

$$I^s = \gamma'\psi(p_B),$$

where γ' could be in principle different from γ. Equation (40) is almost what is needed for *Step 4* but not quite: observe that (40) does not fully express outputs as an explicit function of equilibrium prices because $\gamma = \gamma(B)$. In order to obtain outputs as functions of equilibrium prices alone, one must also find out simultaneously the equilibrium value of $\gamma = \gamma^*(B)$. This is "fixed point" problem, since for each given p_B, γ depends on B while for each p_B, B depends on γ. This is solved in Step 4, which follows, by a simple "fixed point" argument.

Recall that the economy has increasing returns which are external to the firm, and the parameter γ is assumed in (16) to increase with the level of output of B (and potentially also I). For example[18]:

$$\gamma = \gamma(B) = B^\sigma, \quad \sigma < 1. \tag{41}$$

At an equilibrium equations (40) and (41) must be satisfied simultaneously, i.e.

$$\gamma = [\gamma \cdot \phi(p_B)]^\sigma \tag{42}$$
$$= \gamma^\sigma \phi(p_B)^\sigma, \quad \text{or} \quad \gamma^{1-\sigma} = \phi(p_B)^\sigma$$

so that

$$\gamma = \phi(p_B)^{\sigma/(1-\sigma)}.$$

Therefore at an equilibrium (40) and (41) imply a relation between the output of B and p_B. If one assumes that I has external economies as well (which is not necessary for the Results), then one could have a similar expression for I:

$$B^s = \phi(p_B)^{1/(1-\sigma)}.$$
$$I^s = \psi(p_B)^{1/(1-\sigma')}. \tag{43}$$

Note that

$$\text{when } \sigma > 1, \quad \theta = 1/1 - \sigma < 0 \tag{44}$$

so that:

Lemma 2

When $\sigma > 1$, the partial equilibrium supply function of each firm producing B is an increasing function of the price of B, p_B. However, due to the external economies of scale, as the total output of B increases within the region this leads to drops in the price p_B across equilibria, since $\phi(p_B)^{1/(1-\sigma)}$ is a decreasing function of the price p_B. Note that since $\sigma > 1$,

$$\text{as} \quad \sigma \to 1, \quad \theta \to -\infty. \tag{45}$$

---

[18] This is an example. In general $\gamma = \gamma(B^*, I^*)$. The general case admits a similar solution, at the cost of more notation.

p_B

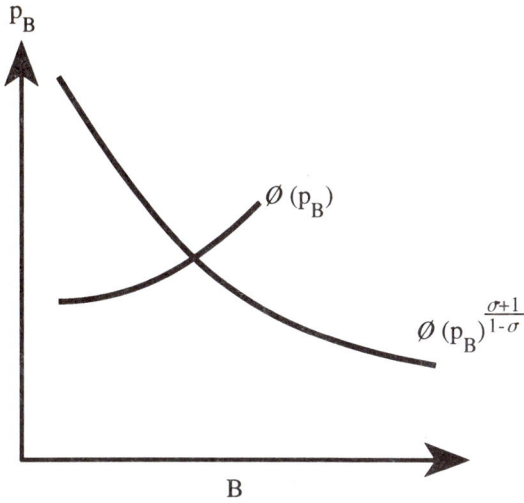

$\emptyset\,(p_B)$

$\emptyset\,(p_B)^{\frac{\sigma+1}{1-\sigma}}$

B

Fig. 5. Each firm faces an upward cost curve. Howerer, the sector B as a whole faces a downward cost curve due to external economies of scale.

Proof

This follows directly: $\phi(p_B)$ is an increasing function of p_B for each fixed γ, but from (44), $\theta = 1/1 - \sigma < 0$, so that increases in total output across equilibria leads to lower prices, see Figure 5.   □

The next step is *Step 5:* to produce the "resolving equation" for the two region model. To solve the model we now consider the market clearing condition in B. At a world equilibrium, the B market must clear so that:

$$B^{d,1}(p_B + t) - B^{s,1}(p_B + t) = B^{s,2}(p_B) - B^{d,2}(p_B),$$

defining the implicit function

$$F(p_B, t) = B^{d,1}(p_B + t) - B^{s,1}(p_B + t) - B^{s,2}(p_B) + B^{d,2}(p_B) = 0. \tag{46}$$

From (18), (19), (21), (32) and (43), equation (46) is a function of the variable p_B alone, which we call a "resolving" equation for this model. Solving the equation $F = 0$ gives the equilibrium values of p_B. Finally Step 6 consists of showing that the equilibrium values of all other variables can be computed from that of p_B. From (32) one obtains l_1 and l_2; from this and (38), (39) one obtains L_1 and K_1; from (22) one obtains r and w in each region; B^s and I^s are obtained in each region from (43). Demand for B and I in each region is obtained from (18) and (19). The model is thus solved. This completes the proof of Proposition 1.   □

The following result has two parts. The first part (i) shows that under the conditions, increasing returns to scale defeat the optimal tariff argument since a tariff on imports leads to lower terms of trade for the importing country. For the second part, assume that $\mu = 1$, so that $B^d = wL$, and that β is small, $\beta < \alpha$; these assumptions are *not* necessary and are *not* used to prove that the terms of trade of the importing region worsen after the tariff. They are only made to simplify the proof of the second part of the Proposition, (ii), namely that the importing regions' welfare decreases after the tariff – other assumptions could be made leading to the same results.

Proposition 3

Consider a world economy as formalized above, in which both regions produce B under condition of external economies of scale. The demand for imports of B by region 1 decreases with world prices of B, and the exporting region, 2, has strong external economies of scale in B:

$$\gamma = \gamma(B) = B^\sigma, \quad \text{with } \sigma > 1,$$

and $\partial X_B^{s,2}/\partial p_B < 0$ is relatively large in absolute value. Then (i) no tariff can improve the terms of trade of the importing region over and above those which the region achieves under free trade, and (ii) the welfare of the importing region is lower with a tariff than without.

Proof

Part (i) first. It is useful to recall first the standard argument for optimal tariffs dicussed above in Section 8.1; this will be only used here as an illustration and to aid intuition. The formal proof is given after this example.

Example 4

Define simple linear functions for home supply and demand, respectively $D = a - b\tilde{p}$, and $Q = e + f\tilde{p}$, so that the demand for imports in $D - Q = (a - e) - (b + f)\tilde{p}$, and define similarly a linear foreign export supply $(Q + - D^*) = g + hp_w$, where p_w is the world price, and $p_w + t = \tilde{p}$. In a world equilibrium imports must equal exports:

$$(a - e) - (b + f)(p_w + t) = g + hp_w. \tag{47}$$

Solving equation (47) for $t=0$ gives p_f the world price without tariffs. Then a tariff takes the world price to $p_w = p_f - t(b+f)/(b+f+h)$ and the internal price to $\tilde{p} = p_f + th/(b+f+h)$. Note that if all parameters are positive, then $p_f < \tilde{p}$, and $p_w < p_f$, implying that the tariff raises the internal price p_f and lowers the world price p_w. Unter this conditions it is easy to see that a positive tariff exists that makes the country better off, because the welfare gains from a tariff obtain from an increase of imports at lower prices, see Section 8.1. Matters change if the economies have increasing returns: in that case the parameters can change sign, for example, if $f < 0$ and is sufficiently large in absolute value, then after the tariff the world price p_w can be higher than p_f. Terms of trade therefore worsen for the country who imposes the tariff, and the gains from the tariff are lost, because world prices increase with respect to domestic prices, while the losses from distortions remain.

I now formalize this example within the equilibrium model of trade defined in this Appendix. The intuition is the same, but it is carried out rigorously using the "resolving equation" and the implicit function theorem.

One studies first the changes in the terms of trade as a function of the tariff t, and shows that the tariff leads to higher rather than lower world prices so that the importing country has better terms of trade without tariffs. By the implicit function theorem from (46):

$$\partial p_B/\partial t = \frac{-\partial F/\partial t}{\partial F/\partial p_B}$$

$$= \frac{-\partial(B^{d,1} - B^{s,1})/\partial(p_B + t)}{[\partial(B^{d,1} - B^{s,1})/\partial(p_B + t)] + [\partial(B^{d,2} - B^{s,2})/\partial p_B]} \tag{48}$$

By the assumptions $\partial(B^{d,1} - B^{s,1})/\partial(p_B + t) < 0$ and therefore the numerator of (48) is positive. The denominator is positive by the assumptions on foreign supply, because due to economies of scale $(\partial X_B^{s,1}/\partial p_B) = \partial(B^{s,2} - B^{d,2})/\partial p_B$ is negative and relatively large (see Lemma 2 above). Therefore, by (48) $\partial p_B/\partial t > 0$: this means that, in a new equilibrium after the tariff t is imposed, the world price p_B increases, so that the importer's terms of trade worsen as stated in (i). The optimal tariff argument is therefore defeated.

Part (ii) next. One shows that lower terms of trade lead region 1 to a lower welfare level. Since in the world equilibrium with tariffs the world price p_B increases, so does the domestic price which is $p_B + t$. Since the importing economy has increasing returns in the B sector, this increase in p_B after the tariff could only be associated to a lower domestic output of the good B. Furthermore, since the exports of the exporting region decrease with prices, the imports of B by region 1 must have decreased as well. Therefore in the new equilibrium the domestic consumption of good B, B^d, is lower in region 1. Finally, consider region 1's consumption of good I. By Walras' law (19), $I^d = rK$. Now by (32) when $\beta < \alpha$, as p_B increases l_2 decreases; by (22) this implies that r decreases as well implying that $I^d = rK$ decreases after the tariff as well. Since both the consumption of B and the consumption of I decrease at home after the tariff in the importing country, the welfare of the importing country decreases after the tariff, completing the proof of Proposition 3. □

References

1. Amelung T (1991) Tropical Deforestation as an International Economic Problem. Paper presented at the Egon Sohmen Foundation Conference on Economic Evolution and Environmental Concern, Linz Austria, August 30–31
2. Barbier EB, Burger JC, Markandya A (1991) The Economic of Tropical Deforestation. AMBIO 20(2):55–58
3. Binkley CS, Vincent JR (1990) Forest based Industrialization: A Dynamic perspective. World Bank Forest Policy Issues Paper, The World Bank, Washington D.C.
4. Chichilnisky G (1981) Terms of Trade and Domestic Distribution: Export Led Growth with Abundant Labor. Journal of Development Economics 8:163–192
5. Chichilnisky G (1986) A General Equilibrium Theory of North-South Trade, Chapter 1, Equilibrium Analysis, Essays in Honor of Kenneth Arrow. Cambridge University Press, pp 3–56
6. Chichilnisky G (1994) North South Trade and the Global Environment. American Economic Review, Volume 84, No. 4, September, 851-874
7. Chichilnisky G (1992) North-South Trade and the Dynamics of Renewable Resources. Working Paper, Columbia University, Structural Change and Economics Dynamics, 1993, December, 4 (2):219–248
8. Chichilnisky G (1992) Trading Blocks with External Economies of Scale. Working Paper, Columbia University, also in "Strategies for Trade Liberalization in the Americas", in *Trade Liberalization in the Western Hemisphere,* IDB-ECLAC, 1995, p 165–188
9. Chichilnisky G, Heal G (1987) The Evolving International Economy. Cambridge University Press
10. Dadzie, Kenneth (1991) Accelerating the Development Process: Challenges for National and International Policies in the 1990s. Report by Secretary General of UNCTAD to UNTAD VIII, United Nations Conference on Trade and Development, United Nations, New York
11. Ethier WJ (1982) Decreasing Costs in International Trade and Frank Graham's Argument for Protection. Econometrica 50/5:1243–1267
12. Graham F (1923) Some Aspects of Protection Further Considered. Quarterly Journal of Economics 37:199–227
13. Hyde WF, Neumann DH (1991) Forest Economics in Brief-with Summary Observations for Policy Analysis. Draft Report, Agricultural and Rural Development, the World Bank, Washington D.C
14. Jacobs J (1985) Cities and the Wealth of Nations. Random House
15. Kennan J, Riezman R (1988) Do Big Countries Win Tariff Wars. International Economic Review 29/1:81–85
16. Kennan J, Riezman R (1990) Optimal Tariff Equilibria with Customs Unions. Canadian Journal of Economics XXIII/1:70–83
17. Krugman P, Obstfelt M (1988) International Economics. Scott, Foresman and Company, Illinois Boston London

18. Lerner A (1936) The symmetry between import and export taxes. Economica 3:306–313
19. Mathews, RCO (1950) Reciprocal Demand and Increasing Returns. Review of Economic Studies 17:149–158
20. Meade J (1952) The Geometry of International Trade. George Allen and Unwin, London
21. Meade J (1955) The Theory of Customs Unions. North-Holland Publishing Company, Amsterdam
22. Meade J (1971) The Theory of Indicative Planning. Allen and Unwin, London
23. Metzler, L (1949) Tariffs the terms of trade and distribution of national income. Journal of Political Economy 57:1–29
24. Nicholson W (1978) Microeconomic Theory. The Dryden Press, Hinsdale, Illinois
25. Riezman R (1985) Customs Unions and the Core. Journal of Internaltional Economics 19:355–365
26. Viner J (1936) The Customs Union Issue. Carnegie Endowment for International Peace, New York, 405 West 117th Street, N.Y.
26. Viner J (1937) Studies in the Theory of International Trade. Harper, New York

The (Not Wholly Satisfactory) State of the Theory of Foreign Direct Investment and the Multinational Enterprise[1]

EDWARD M. GRAHAM

Institute for International Economics, 11 DuPont Circle NW, Washington, DC 20036-1207, USA

Abstract

We examine the state of the theory of foreign direct investment and multinational enterprises with a view to exploring what territory this theory leaves substantially unexplored. The main point that we show is that there is much unexplored territory. The task of explaining why firms become multinational is far from finished.

1 Introduction

Foreign direct investment (FDI) – the major (but not exclusive) mode by which multinational enterprises (MNEs) extend their span of control of business activities internationally – has been called the "neglected twin of trade"[2]. But if FDI has indeed been neglected, it has been only by the academic world; much of the rest of society, including not least the MNEs themselves, but also the governments of most major nations, pays much attention to FDI. At present, in fact, many governments invest substantial resources actively seeking to attract FDI into their economies, such governments include those of nations that were once quite hostile to MNEs, notably China, Mexico, Russia and other former states of the Soviet Union, and well as of source of other nations. Some governments that until very recently have been hostile or, at least, ambivalent towards FDI, e.g., India, Indonesia, Korea, and Brazil, now are showing signs of changing their minds and liberalizing their traditionally restrictive policies.

Indeed, the only major national government that has arguably become less liberal in its official attitudes towards inward FDI is that of the United States, the very same government that for years has extolled other nations to adopt liberal

---

[1] Copyright © Institute for International Economics. An earlier version of this article was presented at the Conference on the Globalization of the World Economy, Centro Interdipartimentale di Economia Internazionale (CIDEI), Universita di Roma "La Sapienza", Rome, Italy, October 27–28, 1994.

[2] Julius 1990.

policies. This anomaly is due to the fact that a significant fraction of economic activity in the United States came under foreign control during a very short period of time, the six years from 1986 through 1991. Certain US constituencies, and members of the US Congress whom they represent, have not wholly digested the new competition that this has brought into the domestic economy.

With respect to the MNEs themselves, during the second half of the 1980s they created a boom in FDI activity that was virtually without precedent. Whereas at yearend 1985 the total stock of FDI worldwide, reported by the United Nations from the statistics supplied to the International Monetary Fund by national governments on inward direct investment, was $ 745.8 billion, by 1992 yearend the stock had risen to $ 1.948.1 billion, an increase of 2.6 times in just seven years.[3] This "boom" appears to be but one of several that have occurred over the last century or so.[4] Indeed, one challenge to those who hope to explain FDI is why it has flowed so irregularly. As will be developed shortly, the response to this challenge is not to date particularly satisfactory.

We should note that there was an earlier "boom" in FDI of major proportion that occurred from the late 1950s until 1967 or so; this was fueled largely by the international expansion of the activities of US-based manufacturing and petroleum firms. During the twenty years or so from the end of this earlier "boom" until the beginning of the most recent one, FDI activity was relatively quiescent world-wide, albeit that what might be described as a "minisurge" occurred in the period between the two oil shocks. The "boom" of 1985–92, unlike that of the 1950s/1960s, involved firms from dozens of home nations, no one of which was dominant in terms of outward flows of direct investment. Indeed, one feature was the large amount of direct investment that flowed *into* the United States, which had been the dominant source of such investment throughout the earlier boom.

A number of characteristics of FDI, additional to the fact that it has occurred in waves, bear mention in this introductory section.

Although the number of firms that could be reasonably classified as "multinational" increased substantially in both the "booms" just identified (and especially so, it would seem, during the second one), FDI remains concentrated in a relatively small set of activities. US statistics for both outward and inward FDI (which are more detailed than for any other nation), indicate that the proportion of FDI in the US manufacturing sector is much greater than the value-added contribution of this sector to the whole economy, and within manufacturing FDI is

---

[3] UNCTAD 1994, Annex table 3. There are some inconsistencies in the definition and coverage of FDI in national statistics.

[4] Alas, however, accurate detailed statistics on international capital flows have been kept only since the 1950s or later in most countries, and detailed figures on FDI and the activities of MNEs exist only in a handful of countries (and, furthermore, these are available in their present detail only back to the 1970s or later). Thus, what is known from earlier "booms" of FDI must be inferred from aggregate data or gleaned from case histories of the experiences of individual investors. On this, see Corley 1994, Jones 1994, and Wilkins 1994.

concentrated in relatively few industries, notably chemicals and pharmaceuticals, transport equipment (mostly autos), electronics (including, computers), nonelectrical machinery, and nonferrous metals. The proportion of FDI in nonmanufacturing sectors has grown during the past ten years, but even so this is concentrated in relatively few industries, e.g., banking and other financial services. By contrast, FDI in the natural resource industries, perhaps the easiest category of direct investment to explain, shrank significantly as a proportion of total FDI during the past decade.

FDI certainly does *not* appear to represent a flow of capital from areas that are relatively well endowed with capital to ones that are not, the vast bulk of FDI during the recent "boom" indeed flowed within the so-called "triad" of western Europe (the EU plus EFTA), Japan, and non-Hispanic North America (Canada and the United States). Furthermore, much of the FDI in the triad is concentrated in the same industries irrespective of the home country, e.g., Germany is both home and host to considerable FDI in the chemical and auto industries, as is the United States. These last facts pose particular difficulties for those economists who tend to see FDI purely as an international factor movement that can be explained in Heckscher/Ohlin terms (i.e., a flow of capital from areas of low return on capital caused by relative abundance to areas of higher such return caused by relative capital scarcity). However, there does appear at the moment to be an upsurge in FDI activity (the beginning of a third "boom"?) wherein the principal recipients are the rapidly industrializing nations, notably those of east Asia but also including some Latin American countries. It is a bit too early to assess the extent of this latest development.

A related and long-standing issue is whether FDI is in net a substitute for exports of the home nation or a complement to these. Factor proportions theory would, of course, predict the former.[5] Most empirical research has supported, however, the latter, complementary relationship, albeit anecdotal evidence suggests that at a disaggregated level, it can go either way, i.e., FDI can under some circumstances act as a substitute for exports but under other circumstance, act as a complement.[6] Under any circumstance, MNEs account for some very large fraction of world trade. For example, over 40% of both US exports and US imports of merchandise are accounted for by transactions of US-based firms with foreign affiliates or by exports and imports of US-based affiliates of non-US based firms to and from the home country of the parent organization.

With these few summary facts in mind, we proceed to examine the state of the theory of FDI and the MNE, with a view to exploring what territory this theory leaves substantially unexplored. The main point that will be emphasized is that

---

[5] The classic article on this subject is Mundell 1957.

[6] See e.g. Lipsey and Weiss 1981 and 1984, Blomström, Lipsey, and Kulchyck 1988, Buigues and Jacquemin 1994, and Graham 1994.

there is in fact much unexplored territory; the task of explaining why firms become multinational is thus far from finished.

2 OLI and the Fuzzy Edge[7]

Within the field of international business, it has become virtually mandatory for young scholars to cite what is variously known as the "OLI" or "electic" paradigm of FDI and the MNE (these are both the same thing) when discussing direct investment or multinational enterprises. Associated with John Dunning, this paradigm is aptly named, for it is indeed eclectic and it is even a paradigm.[8] The dictionary definition of the latter is "a pattern, or a model". As will be developed, the first definition is the more apt; the eclectic paradigm is more a taxonomical description of a pattern than a model.

This paradigm is, by Dunning own statement, an effort to synthesize a number of different strands of thinking about FDI. The essence of the synthesis lies in the letters "O", "L", and "I".

The first letter, "O", stands for ownership advantages. These are firm-specific assets, including intangible ones such as proprietary or trade-secret technologies, that individual firms might possess that give them competitive advantages over rival firms. That firms might possess such assets was first systematically explored by Dunning himself (1958) and Hymer (1959). The possible existence of firm-specific advantages has remained at the core of theoretical treatment of FDI ever since.

Dunning's 1958 research reported empirical findings about the activities of UK affiliates of US-owned firms, many of which were recently established. These affiliates, he found, tended to be more productive and, by a variety of other measures, to outperform their domestically owned UK rivals. He attributed the differential performance to ownership advantages possessed by the US-owned affiliates not shared with their local rivals. Dunning also found evidence that with the passage of time the British firms tended to catch up with the US-owned affiliates.

Hymer postulated that in order for a firm to operate multinationally, it must possess some sort of advantage over rival firms in national markets outside its home market. The specific advantages identified by Hymer were (i) economies of scale that could be realized by integrating operations owned by a single firm across more than one national market and (ii) "marketing skills".

---

[7] Portions of this section also appear in Edward M. Graham, "What can the Theory of Foreign Direct Investment Tell Us About the Low Level of Foreign Firm Participation in the Economy of Japan", paper presented at the Wharton School, University of Pennsylvania, October 7, 1994.

[8] The eclectic paradigm has evolved rather considerably over the years; see e.g., Dunning 1980, and 1993, pp. 76–86.

Most authors now would include as ownership advantages other intangible assets such as proprietary product and process technologies, ability to create new technologies, organizational and managerial skills beyond those associated with marketing, and intellectual property not technological in nature, e.g., well recognized brand names. Dunning includes also what he terms "advantages of common governance", including advantages that established enterprises might have over new entrants (accumulated learning effects, economies of scope, ability to obtain inputs on favorable terms, etc.) and advantages "which specifically arise because of multinationality", including ability to shift production from relative high to relatively low cost locations.

The second letter (L) of the eclectic paradigm stands for location advantages, which can be thought of in two ways: (i) home nation location advantages, i.e., those characteristics of a location that might cause non-multinational firms operating there initially to develop ownership advantages enabling multinational operations, and (ii) host nation advantages, i.e., those characteristics of a nation that might cause foreign firms already possessing ownership advantages to locate economic activities there in preference to locations in other nations.

Exploration of home nation location advantages in a systematic way was first motivated by investigation of why, during the 1950s and 1960s, large US-based manufacturing firms both were leading exporters of goods embodying new and complex technologies and leading direct investors. Vernon (1966) and (1974) in particular explored a pattern whereby US multinational manufacturing firms first would export goods embodying new technologies from the United States but later establish (via FDI) local manufacture of the goods in foreign (at the time, mostly European) countries. This pattern suggested the "product life cycle" hypothesis of international trade and investment which, *inter alia,* offered reasons why technology-intensive consumer and capital goods were so often first commercial-ized in the United States and later produced in other advanced nations. For the former (consumer goods), the reasoning was that *per capita* incomes (then) were significantly higher in the United States than elsewhere and that, because these goods were characterized by high income elasticities of demand, total demand in the United States was much higher than elsewhere. This, it was argued, led to demand-induced innovation. For capital goods, it was reasoned that artisan class labor was relatively scarce in the United States and, hence, there was an induced demand for new capital goods that substituted for this class of labor. This last helped in turn to explain why *per capita* US incomes were so much higher than in other industrialized nations, in spite of the fact that the US labor force that was not evidently more skilled or better educated than that of other advanced nations: Capital goods embodying new technologies that substituted for labor enabled high marginal labor productivity to be achieved in the United States even though the workers utilized to operate this capital were not necessarily highly skilled.

In a fully integrated world economy, globally-oriented firms might be expected to seek out production locations where host nation advantages best meshed with ownership advantages to give the firm its maximum overall advantage. By classical reasoning, these local conditions would be determined by relative factor prices as well as transportation and other transactions costs, firms would locate production operations so as to minimize costs of supplying major markets, exporting and importing both intermediate and final goods to achieve the minimization. Indeed, Wells (1972) and others postulated that in the long run trade patterns created by multinational firms would come to coincide with those predicted by Heckscher-Ohlin theory. One consequence would be that the locus of innovation would no longer coincide with the locus of production; each type would come to be located where relative factor prices most favored it, and presumably these would be different locations. Wells indeed saw multinational enterprises eventually entering third world nations *en masse,* transferring to those nations production of good embodying labor intensive production processes. But while this has happened to some extent in certain industries (e.g., apparel, electronics assembly), it has not happened nearly to the extent that Wells and other writers might have predicted during the early 1970s.

In a recent paper, Katseli (1991), building upon Krugman (1991), explores why this is so. She concludes that the main reason is that host nation location advantage isn't principally determined by relative factor prices. Rather, FDI (other than the "resource seeking" variety, i.e., FDI that occurs in extractive industries) is drawn to areas characterized by access to markets of minimum necessary size and by low uncertainty, high absolute (as opposed to relative) efficiency of inputs, and "thick market externatilities" (explained below). According to Katseli, these should be treated not as independent factors but as interdependent ones: e.g., thick market externalities probably cannot exist in markets of low absolute size.

Thick market externalities occur when there exists sufficient geographic clustering of business activities that opportunities for networking among business are generated. The networking creates what are in effect external economies of scope (or, in some cases, external economies of scale) for firms operating within the cluster. For example, an operation might be located in an area where opportunities exist for obtaining numerous specialized inputs from competent subcontractors, none of which could be sustained by that one operation alone. Availability of a pool of workers with specialized skills (as opposed to high general levels of education) might also figure in the location decision. Katseli concludes that where thick market externalities figure heavily, "... investors take ... into acount their expectations of how fast other investors will follow suit. They may then decide to wait until enough investors have jumped in." This might help to explain the sectoral and temporal clustering of FDI that has been observed in specific national markets (Knickerbocker 1974, Yu and Ito 1988).

Thick market externalities are of particular importance in technologically dynamic industries, where one element is a common pool of rapidly changing knowledge wherein new developments are passed by R & D personnel largely through informal contact. To keep abreast of developments, firms thus find it advantageous to be located in close proximity to other firms utilizing the same pool.

We shall return to some of these concepts in the fourth section of this paper. But, for now, we continue with the eclectic paradigm.

The third letter (I) of the eclectic paradigm stands for "internalization". The relevant issue with respect to internalization is, why do firms seek to exploit ownership advantages via FDI rather than other modes of operating international-ly, e.g., licensing to indigenous producers or exportation through independent distributors? The concept of internalization, at least as it pertains to the multinational enterprise, was introduced by Buckley and Casson (1976). But the concept dates to Coase (1937) and Buckley and Casson's treatment is based upon refinements by Williamson (1970 and 1973).

The essence of internalization is that a firm chooses to work firm-specific assets (i.e., ownership advantages) internally – that is, via operations that are integrated within one organization – because it is more efficient to do so rather than to work these via arm's length relationships with independent vendors and marketers or via simply selling the assets to rival firms. Indeed, because this lattermost alternative might seem particularly attractive as a means of servicing a foreign market where doing business requires knowledge and organizational skills specific to the market not possessed by the firm seeking to work the assets, one might expect licensing of technologies and other intangible assets to be the dominant mode of international commerce. Servicing of the foreign market via internalization does make sense, however, if the gains capturable by the firm via internalization clearly dominate the learning and startup costs associated with direct participation in the foreign market. The potential gains derive from either reduced transactions costs somewhat broadly defined (including costs associated with moral hazard) or reduced opportunity from internalization.

Dunning (1994) lists seven categories of transactions costs that can be minimized or avoided via internalization. These are (1) search and negotiation costs; (2) costs of broken contracts (including litigation of these); (3) costs associated with buyer uncertainty about nature or value of inputs; (4) costs associated with lack of futures markets; (5) costs associated with government intervention in markets; (6) costs associated with conditions of sale; and (7) costs associated with moral hazard and adverse selection.

As an example of the second (opportunity costs), suppose that Firm "A" perceived that transfer of technology might ultimately give firm "B" the ability to compete in markets where firm "A" currently is able to generate rents. In this case, FDI might be then preferred to licensing in order to preempt a rival from gaining access to proprietary technology, on grounds that such access would reduce future profits (this expected loss would be the specific "opportunity cost"). Dunning (1994) also considers loss of the ability of a firm to extract rents as a result of market power to be an opportunity cost.

A variant on the internalization hypothesis is offered by Cantwell (1990) that he terms "technological accumulation". The essential idea is that when large business organizations internalize operations that are technologically complex, they develop variations on these operations that are *sui generis* to their own organizations. For example, each of several firms might offer substitutable variants of a product embodying advanced technologies. Although the products are close substitutes, because they are technologically complex, each firm in developing its own variant likely would take approaches to product design and production that were somewhat different from its rivals. The result would be differing production processes using specialized and noninterchangeable capital goods. Also, specific know-how associated with production of the product might differ considerably from firm to firm. Thus, very specific know-how of substantial value to one firm might not be of equal value to another firm, even if it produced a substitutable product.

The eclectic paradigm is, as already suggested, more a taxonomy than a model; its major strength is that it accounts for almost all known factors that might cause a particular firm to become multinational, and organizes these in a way that is intellectually useful. A blend of what might be termed "classical" industrial economics (i.e., industrial organization theory as it stood prior to the incorporation of elements of game theory) and the theory of the firm, the paradigm is, as suggested by Dunning himself, more descriptive than it is normative, e.g., it is useful as a means of describing why firms that are multinational came to be that way but it is less useful as a means of predicting what directions these firms will take in the future. Katesli's treatment of host nation advantages and Cantwell's variation on the internalization hypothesis are particularly useful in that both introduce elements of what has come to be termed "path dependence" into the eclectic paradigm. Path dependence, a concept that is rather new in economics but rapidly becoming part of mainstream thinking, suggests that the current state of an economic system can be a function of the "path" taken to achieve that state, i.e., that the history of the system matters.[9] It follows that the possible states of the system in the future are constrained by (but not necessarily completely determined by) the history of the system. Thinking about path dependence in economics is still in its infancy, and both the Katseli and Cantwell formulations are at this point themselves more descriptive than normative, but they quite possibly are at the leading edge of what could become an exciting new field of inquiry.[10]

Having said this, it must be noted that the eclectic paradigm falls short on several counts even by the criterion of how well it explains the existing state of the world. The paradigm does not, for example, well explain the "waves" of foreign

---

[9] Thus, economic systems are not Markovian; the current state of the system (time $t = T$) depends upon states -visited in the past, and not simply the state of the system at time "$T - 1$".

[10] Casson 1991 suggests some of the directions research in international business might go down the "path dependant" path.

direct investment that have occurred in the post-World War II era, as described in the introductory section of this essay; nor is there much in the paradigm to explain the clustering of FDI in certain industries.

Explanations of FDI and the behavior of MNEs that are based on dynamic models of oligopoly do slightly better on both counts than does the eclectic paradigm but, as will be developed, these models are far from wholly satisfactory. We turn next to these.

3 Models of Interfirm Rivalry and FDI[11]

Models of FDI based on the dynamics of interfirm rivalry are closely akin to "strategic" models of international trade associated with Barbara Spencer, William Brander, and Paul Krugman, but the FDI models actually have a somewhat longer lineage. But whereas early versions of the FDI models tended to be fairly qualitative, strategic models have been from the outset mathematical. For example, Vernon's "product life cycle" hypothesis can be viewed as a model of rivalry as well as one of locational advantage – rivalry created by local firms induces exporters to themselves become local by means of FDI – but the development of this idea is qualitative.

Also very qualitative in nature is a model implicit in a frequently cited article of Hymer and Rowthorne (1970), in which dynamics of rivalry among MNEs from Europe and the United States would lead to cross investment and consolidation with the ultimate consequence that a few hundred firms would come to dominate world commerce. Indeed, one has to use the term "model" in this context guardedly, because Hymer and Rowthorne never specified exactly how this concentration would come about.

In contrast to Vernon and Hymer and Rowthorne, there have been more recent efforts to make rigorous FDI rivalry models using concepts drawn from noncooperative game theory (e.g., Baer 1984, Onida 1989, Graham 1990). As do their strategic trade counterparts, such "rigorous" FDI models must rely on restricting assumptions that are open to criticism as unrealistic. Nonetheless, the models do seem to be able to help explain some of empirical observable patterns of MNE behavior that, as already noted, the eclectic paradigm does not readily explain.

Four models are discussed here, Knickerbocker's (1973) "follow-the-leader" model, Graham's (1978) "exchange-of-threat" model, Sanna-Randaccio's (1990) "nonprovocative firm growth" model, and Acocella's (1991) "monopolization" model.

---

[11] Portions of this section also appear in Edward M. Graham, "Los determinantes de la inversión extranjera directa teorías alternativas y evidencia internacional" ("The Determinants of Foreign Direct Investment: Theories and Empirical Evidence") *Moneda y Crédito* 194, 1992, pp. 13–49.

All of these models assume that multinational enterprises operate in oligopolistic markets where there are opportunities for the appropriation of economic rents. Why the markets might be oligopolistic in the first place is not generally discussed, although a number of empirical studies show a positive correlation between measures of market concentration and percentage of industry output accounted for by MNEs. In the models, the markets are completely disjoint; that is, they are geographically separate, and outcomes in one geographic market do not directly affect outcomes in any other market (i.e., there is no goods arbitrage linking the markets).

Knickerbocker's model begins by assuming that in some market, there is oligopoly equilibrium among a set of rival firms. (Exactly what type of equilibrium is not specified.) A rivalrous process is then started by one firm making a foreign direct investment. Rival firms in the home market find this to be upsetting because the firm that has made the foreign direct investment (the "first mover") now holds a monopoly position in the new market, and any rents accruing from this position can be used to cross subsidize operations in the home market. Motivated by this fear, the rival firms invest directly in the same foreign market so as to reestablish an equilibrium.

Knickerbocker did not develop this model in a formal way by advancing deductive arguments to suggest if, under some plausible set of assumptions, the follower firms entering the foreign market was indeed a best response to the first mover. Rather, he stated the above scenario as an hypothesis and proceeded to test it empirically, demonstrating that US-based firms in a given industry, when entering foreign markets via FDI, have indeed tended to cluster their first entries into a two or three year period. Similar patters have been discovered for FDI from other nations (Flowers 1976, Yu and Ito 1988). Baer (1984) has attempted a more rigorous formulation of the Knickerbocker model and to test it using Monte Carlo simulations.

Graham (1978) posited something of the opposite situation. Initially, firms operate as monopolists in two markets. One firm chooses to enter the other firm's market by means of FDI, thus breaking the monopoly in that market. The second firm then will find that its optimal response is to enter the first firm's market, whereupon both firms will find it to mutual advantage to cease and desist from rivalrous behavior and to collude so as jointly to appropriate rents from both markets. Graham tested the model using cross-investment between the United States and Europe and found some support for the hypothesis that European direct investment in the United States was stimulated by earlier US direct investment in Europe. In particular, lagged response of European firms to entry into their home markets by US firms seemed to explain why European FDI in the United States tended to be concentrated in many of the same industries as US FDI in Europe.

Although the empirical evidence supporting the Knickerbocker hypothesis is stronger than that supporting the Graham hypothesis, the exchange-of-threat model is capable of being formulated more rigorously than the follow-the-leader model, essentially because in the former the reactive firm finds its situation directly affected by the actions of the first mover whereas in the latter the reactive firm (or firms) must anticipate some future move by the first mover that is threatening (such as predatory pricing in the home market). The exchange-of-threat model is structurally very similar to the "reciprocal dumping" mode of William Brander and Paul Krugman (1984). In both models, for example, firms from different nations are able to enter each other"s markets costlessly, and yet there are absolute barriers to entry to any other firm.

A simple exposition of "exchange of threat" is as follows:[12]

Assume that there are two firms, each operating as a monopolist in its home market; these markets are geographically and politically independent, and there is no goods arbitrage between them. Call one of these home markets A and the other B, and associate with any single subscript of a variable the market indicated by that subscript (e.g., Q_A would be the equilibrium quantity supplied and demanded in market A.) Label the monopoly firms in each of these markets also as A and B, but associate with any double subscript of a variable both the relevant market by the first subscript and the relevant firm by the second subscript (e.g., Q_{AA} would be the equilibrium quantity supplied in market A by firm A, but Q_{AB} would be the quantity supplied in market A by firm B). Also, assume that demand in each market is linear and can be written in inverted form $P_A = A - aQ_A$ for market A and $P_B = B - bQ_B$ for market B. The letters A and B when used alone in an equation (i.e., not as subscripts) will always refer to the market constants rather than as identifiers of the firms or the markets. These and all other equations should be treated as pertaining to one "market period" in a "game" between the two firms that is repeated. (Thus, every variable in what follows implicitly carries a subscript t, $t = 1, 2, \ldots$)

Assume now that firm A has constant marginal cost C_A and firm B has constant marginal cost C_B. If both firms continue to be monopolists in their home markets, equilibrium prices and quantities in these markets will be

$$P_A^m = (A + C_A)/2 \qquad Q_A^m = Q_{AA}^m = (A - C_A)/2a$$

$$P_B^m = (B + C_B)/2 \qquad Q_B^m = Q_{BB}^m = (B - C_B)/2b$$

and the profits of the two firms will be

$$\pi_A^m = (A^2 - 2aC_A + C_A^2)/4a$$

$$\pi_B^m = (B^2 - 2bC_B + C_B^2)/4b,$$

where the superscript m indicates that the equilibrium is one of monopoly.

---

[12] A more thorough development of the model is in Graham 1990.

For sake of simplicity, assume that there are no barriers to FDI (but that trade continues to be impossible!) and that neither firm discounts future profits. This latter allows us to momentarily ignore any transient phenomena that might occur in a dynamic game between the two firms. (In particular, entry can be treated as costless). Let us now assume that firm B enters market A by means of FDI, and that the outcome in this market is a Cournot duopoly. (For this to happen, it must be that $C_A < (A + C_B)/2$.) Total profits in this market will fall and will now be allocated between the two firms as follows:

$$\pi_{AA}^C = (A^2 - 4AC_A + 2AC_B - 4C_AC_B + C_B^2 + 4C_A^2)/9a$$

$$\pi_{AB}^C = (A^2 - 4AC_B + 2AC_A - 4C_AC_B + C_A^2 + 4C_B^2)/9a,$$

where the superscript c indicates a Cournot duopoly.

Firm B gains profit equal to π_{AB}^C and firm B loses profit in the amount $(\pi_A^m - \pi_{AB}^C)$. If $C_A > (A + C_B)/2$, firm A will leave the market. Otherwise, firm A's best response to firm B's entry would be to counter-enter market B. This would reduce firm B's profit in its home market to $\pi_{BB}^C = (B^2 - 4AC_B + 2AC_A - 4C_AC_B + C_A^2 + 4C_B^2)/9b$, and the total gain in profits to firm B would simply be $\Delta\pi = (\pi_{AB}^C + \pi_B^m - \pi_{BB}^C)$. Clearly, by inductive reasoning, firm B would then not enter market A unless $\pi_{AB}^C > (\pi_B^m - \pi_{BB}^C)$, or, written out:

$$(A^2 + 2AC_A - 4AC_B - 4CAC_B + C_A^2 + 4C_B^2)/9a$$
$$> (5B^2 - 8BC_A - 2BC_B + 16C_AC_B - 4C_A^2 - 7C_B^2)/36b.$$

The model thus predicts that if firms do not discount future profits or losses, FDI flows should be two way unless the reacting firm (firm A above) has variable costs above a certain amount.

In the model as depicted above, monopoly in each market is replaced by duopoly, suggesting that the two way FDI flow is unequivocally pro-competitive. It is easy to show, however, that under certain assumptions that are not excessively restrictive, once two way investment has been achieved, it could be profitable for both firms to collude to maximize profits in both markets. The easiest case to exposit is where the two firms have equal costs $(= C)$.[13] Suppose that firm A, having entered market B, does not achieve its full Cournot equilibrium market share immediately, perhaps because of some reluctance of consumers to switch suppliers, but that price does fall quickly to the Cournot level. When the market share of firm A is greater than

$$(B^2 - 2BC - 4C^2 + 4C)/(9B^2 - 36BC - 27C^2)$$

---

[13] This case violates the initial assumption that $C_B < C_A$; the assumption that the two costs are equal is used here simply to avoid algebraic expressions that are very lengthy.

firm A would rather allow price to rise (and quantity demanded to fall) to the monopoly level rather than to achieve a Cournot duopoly outcome. At this point, firm B is in a position to make a deal: the two firms will jointly monopolize the market, with firm A holding the share above, but if firm A attempts to exceed this market share, firm B will allow price to fall to the Cournot level. The outcome of the shared monopoly Pareto-dominates the Cournot outcome, which in turn is a nonrepeated game Nash equilibrium. Thus, the shared monopoly outcome is a subgame perfect Nash equilibrium if the "game" is infinitely repeated (which, presumably, it would be), by the folk theorem of noncooperative game theory.[14] This repeated game equilibrium, one should note, is one where firm A (the "foreign firm" in market B) holds in perpetuity a market share of less than 50%. A similar situation holds in market A but with the roles of firms A and B reversed.

Sanna-Randaccio's model is something of an alternative to the exchange-of-threat model as an explanation for two way direct investment between the United States and Europe being concentrated in the same industries. The model borrows from Penrose, and assumes that for behavioral reasons firms seek to maximize total profits rather than profits per unit of capital (i.e., rate of return). Firms in oligopoly industries find, however, that they cannot expand at home without disrupting local oligopoly equilibria; e.g., even efforts to increase market share marginally might change the nature of the home market game from a repeated cooperative game (wherein rents are jointly maximized) to Cournot rivalry (wherein most rent would be bid away). However, these fimrs might find that they can gain market share in foreign markets up to some limit without provoking any reaction from local rivals. For example, the MNEs might play a Cournot strategy against the local rivals and, unlike the case in the normal Cournot game, these rivals might hold output constant in an effort to maintain rents. Thus, the local firms will in effect behave collectively as a dominant firm price leader, and allow market share to erode to some point beyond which dominant firm price leadership becomes a losing proposition. Hence, multinational enterprises from a diverse set of home markets will, via FDI, appropriate small shares of foreign markets. No established local firm in these markets will take retaliatory action so long as these shares remain small: the best response of large firms in these markets is not to respond at all. Sanna-Randaccio postulated that this situation could exist reciprocally: dominant firms in the United States would take a small market share in Europe, while their European firms would take a small market share in the United States, each without provoking retaliatory action on the part of the other set of firms.

Thus, both the Sanna-Randaccio model and the Graham model are essentially ones to explain two way FDI theoretically and, in particular, to explain how within one industry, MNEs from the United States might hold a minority market share in Europe while their European rivals hold a similar minority market share in the

---

[14] A number of versions of the folk theorem are developed in Fudenberg and Maskin 1986.

United States. How do they fare empirically? To this author's knowledge, no empirical tests have been reported other than those appearing in Graham 1978. This perhaps is surprising given the large quantity of two way FDI that has flowed in the intervening years, and it would seem that further empirical work might at this time be fruitful.

Acocella's model essentially is based on the premise that if appropriation and preservation of rents is what FDI is all about, why should firms play complicated strategic games when they instead can merge and thus create monopolies (or, at least, high levels of firm concentration) in industries in which joint appropriation of rent is facilitated)? Although theoretical in nature, Acocella's model is based on the observation that much of FDI among the developed nations of Europe, North America, and Japan during the 1980s was achieved via merger and acquisition rather than greenfields investment. The hypothesis that merger and acquisition occurs to create monopolies or collusive oligopolies is, of course, a very old one, but one that has largely been used to explain merger and acquisition activity within a single national market.

As explanators of FDI, models based on interfirm rivalry seem to have some power to explain the clustering of FDI (and, hence, they help perhaps to explain why it occurs in waves) as well as why there is quite a lot of intraindustry FDI worldwide. Fundamentally, however, the models have two shortcomings, viz. (i) they depend some "triggering event" that is, with the possible exception of Sanna-Randaccio, external to the model and (ii) with the exception of Acocella, they fail to explain why FDI is chosen in preference to other modes of international business, e.g., exports. On the latter, it is worth noting that the "follow-the-leader", "exchange-of-threat", and "nonprovocative firm growth" models remain essentially unchanged if FDI is replaced by exports; the models address why firms might seek to work foreign markets, not why they choose FDI to do so. Of course, the choice of FDI over other modes of international business is the central issue addressed in the internalization compartment of the eclectic model.

4 Into the Woods[15]

In this section we return to the concept of clustering of economic activity that was touched upon in section 2 with the discussion of Katseli (1991). The effort is made here to expand and generalize this discussion by examining economic geography

---

[15] This section of this essay is not to be confused with a Stephen Sondheim play by the same name; portions of this section also appear in Edward M. Graham, "Canadian Direct Investment Abroad and the Canadian Economy: Some Theoretical and Empirical Considerations", in Stephen Globerman, editor, *Canadian-Based Multinationals* (Calgary, Alberta: the University of Calgary Press, for Industry Canada, 1994).

theory somewhat more broadly than was done in the earlier section and to attempt to link this with the eclectic paradigm of FDI.

Economic geography theory is to a large extent concerned with explaining the reasons for the existence of geographic clusters of economic activity. Such clusters do exist – the very existence of cities is one demonstration of clustering – and efforts have been made for a long time to explain their existence. But recently developed ideas do not concern themselves with the existence of cities *per se,* but rather the propensity of specialized and/or related activities to be clustered in certain locations. For example, the US semiconductor industry is very heavily concentrated in the famous "Silicon Valley" area south of San Francisco (but smaller clusters exist in other areas, e.g., around Austin, Texas, Durham, North Carolina, and Orlando, Florida), whereas the North American auto industry has historically been clustered around Detroit, Michigan and Windsor, Ontario. Indeed, for many categories of product of service, clusters of activity can be identified throughout the world (see, e.g., Porter 1990).

Exactly why, how, and where a cluster initially develops is not fully understood. Within the new theory models have been developed that demonstrate that if, as an initial condition, factors of production are initially uniformly distributed across a geographical space if an activity characterized by localized external economies of scale of sufficient magnitude appears on the scene, at least some of these factors will migrate to one location to create one or more clusters of this activity. However, no such initial condition exists in the real world and, thus, it is difficult on the basis of the theory to predict exactly when and where clusters of entirely new activities will develop. Indeed, the emerging literature on economic geography suggests that, to explain why particular clusters are located where they are, an appeal to historic accident can be as powerful as any appeal to rigorous deduction[16].

Theory does better, however, in explaining the characteristics of an established cluster and how new clusters of an established economic activity arise apart from old ones. For example, an established cluster will tend to be stable as a result of incumbency advantages specific to its location. However, these incumbency advantages are not absolute, and as conditions change, new clusters of the same or similar activities might develop elsewhere.

Whatever the specific reasons why a cluster initially develops in a particular location, as noted in the earlier discussion, the cluster typically owes its existence to "thick market externalities", e.g., localized external economies of scale that enable individual operating units ("plants") to be able to operate at a lower cost if these are located in close geographical proximity to one another than if they are scattered in geographically disperse locations. Such a scale economy must, of course, be distinguished from an internal scale economy, which will govern the optimal size of an individual plant.

---

[16] See, e.g., Krugman 1992.

As noted earlier, one reason why such external scale economies might exist is because firms draw from common pools of specialized factors of production. For example, a plant might require workers possessing specialized skills not employed in other activities, but the plant's requirements for these workers might be subject to some seasonal or cyclical variation. Under these circumstances, there would be an economic reason for managers to locate such a plant where it could hire workers from (or release them into) a pool of individuals possessing the requisite skills. In the absence of such a pool, the firm would either be forced (a) to train new workers every time requirements rose and to lay them off in the knowledge that they would not be available for rehiring when demand picked up, or (b) to retain unused workers during periods of slack demand. Either of these last two alternatives would create transactions costs that would be avoided if the plant were able to draw from (and release into) a common pool as conditions warranted.

But any such existing pool would be located where preexisting plants were located, where workers possessing the specialized skills would be able to sell their services to multiple employers. This would be of advantage to the individual worker because any such worker who happened to be temporarily unemployed would face a lower expected duration of unemployment than if located somewhere where only one potential employer existed. But location in proximity to a cluster of plants would reduce the likely duration of unemployment for any individual worker if fluctuations in activity at each plant were to be statistically independent or even partly so.

Thus, the existence of the pool of workers all by itself creates an external scale advantage to plants that are close enough to draw from the pool (the cost of training workers is minimized) and in addition creates an external scale economy for workers possessing relevant skills (costs associated with being out of work are also minimized). Such external economies of scale, once in place, can be difficult to reproduce elsewhere and hence are one source of the cluster's incumbency advantages.

In addition to pools of specialized factors, the cluster might have associated with it pools of what might be termed complementary activities (e.g., the subcontracting of goods or services necessary to the functioning of the main activities) which create additional localized external scale economies from which the cluster derives additional incumbency advantages.

Common pools of factors of production are not limited to labor pools. A particular economic activity might require, for example, certain specialized non labor inputs where it is more economical for a plant to contract out the service than to maintain an internal capability. This would be especially so if the efficient scale of production of the input were to be greater than the demands of one plant, in which case one supplier would meet the needs of several plants. In the case of activities involving advanced, rapidly changing technology, one input that is often "pooled" is information. The local external scale economy for such an industry results from informal information networking among personnel who work for competing firms but who share information nonetheless.

The advantages created by external scale economies in no way conflict with the possibility that there might be, in a clustered activity, economies of internalization that compel plants to be held under common ownership *as per* the eclectic paradigm. Where there exists for some activity an economy of internalization, there can also exist, at the level of the individual plant, a localized external scale economy. In such a case, plants and related activities might *both* be clustered geographically *and* be operated within a single organization or within a small number of organizations. In the extreme case, a single firm could own a multiple plant operation in a single cluster. Thus, for example, dozens of plants producing automobiles or automotie components are concentrated around Toyota City in the Kansai region of Japan, but the final product is produced by only one firm operating multiple plants. In such a case, the external economies of scale would be entirely internalized within the organization, but they would still be "external" from the perspective of the individual plant.

Incumbency advantages created by external scale economies are reinforced by the fact that a cluster not only supplies goods and services but also demands them. If transportation and other transactional costs increase with distance, such costs are reduced to the extent that the goods and services produced in a cluster are also consumed there. The combined effects of "supply side" incumbency advantages (borne basically of economies of scale) and "demand side" ones (borne basically of logistical advantages) are such that, in formal models of clusters, these clusters become stable equilibria in the spatial coordinates of a suitable cartesian space.[17]

In the theory of economic geography, trade arises as a natural consequence of the clustering of activity: simply put, it is cost-minimizing to produce a particular good or service at one location and to ship the good or service to meet demand in outlying areas. "Outlying areas" can include other clusters of economic activity. Thus, for example, the Nagoya (Toyota City) area of Japan supplies automobiles to Tokyo, even though the latter is a much larger clusters of (other) economic activities than is the former. Likewise, financial services consumed in Nagoya may originate in Tokyo.

The trade thus generated can be in intermediate products. This opens up the possibility that if, in the production of some particular product or service, there exist both internal economies that span the vertical production process and (different) local external scale economies at the various vertical stages of production of the product, one firm might own "upstream" plants at one location and "downstream" plants at some other location, shipping intermediate goods from the former to the latter. And, if the two locations are on opposite sides of a national boundary, the two sets of economies (internalization and localized

---

[17] In formal models, the clusters are concentrated on a single point in a phase-space, obviously not a practical result!

external scale) would give rise to vertical direct investment and to associated cross border trade flows. The trade flows would then be two-way: intermediate goods would flow "downstream", but finished goods would also flow "upstream" to meet the demands of local consumers in the "upstream" cluster. Also, these trade flows would be complementary to the direct investment. Indeed, without the investment, the trade flows would not exist.

As already mentioned, incumbency advantages are neither absolute nor time-invariant. Growth in demand, or changes in transactional costs, can alter the situation such that it becomes economic for a new cluster to develop apart from the original cluster. Indeed, in formal models of clustering, when the accumulated changes reach the point where a new cluster forms, the change is very dramatic: the optimal locations for both of the (now two) cluster, with the result that factors migrate away from the original location and to the new ones.[18]

Mathematical models from which such a result ensues embody concepts from chaos theory.[19] Formally, creation of the new clusters results from bifurcation of equilibrium points at which the clustering takes place. A "bifurcation" is the splitting of a single equilibrium point into several new equilibria (usually three, one of which is unstable). Bifurcations typically occur when the value of some parameter reaches a critical point. In economic geography models, the parameter most offen represents total demand.

A simple case of bifurcation is the period doubling bifurcation that occurs when the parameter α of the logistic function $x_t = \alpha x_{t-1}(1 - x_{t-1})$, a second degree difference equation described in elementary chaos theory, reaches certain critical values and $0 \leq x_0 \leq 1$. For values of α in the range $1 \leq \alpha \leq 3$ and for $0 \leq x_0 \leq 1$, there is one stable (attracting) equilibrium at $x = (\alpha - 1)/\alpha$ and one unstable (repelling) equilibrium at $x = 0$. But, as α increases beyond $\alpha = 3$, a transformation occurs at the point of the stable equilibrium. In the vicinity of $\alpha = 3.24$, two new stable equilibria arise in the immediate vicinity of the original one at $\alpha = (\alpha - 1)/\alpha$ while, simultaneously, the old equilibrium shifts from stable to unstable. The process is as depicted in Diagram 1. As the parameter α increases past the first bifurcation, the loci of the new stable equilibria move away from the original equilibrium point until a new bifurcation occurs, whereupon two new stable equilibria appear in the immediate vicinity of each of the stable equilibria resulting from the previous bifurcation. These formerly stable equilibria again simultaneously become unstable. The sequence of the values of α at which bifurcations occur follows a geometric progression with the parameter of the progression equal to Feigenbaum's constant δ, where $\delta \approx 4.7$. At the point of accumulation of the progression the whole phenomenon becomes chaotic.

---

[18] This assumes that the factors are mobile; obviously, if one factor is immobile (e.g., land), a different result would obtain.

[19] A mathematical introduction to chaos theory is Devaney 1989. A readable (i.e., nonmathematical) introduction is Gleick 1987.

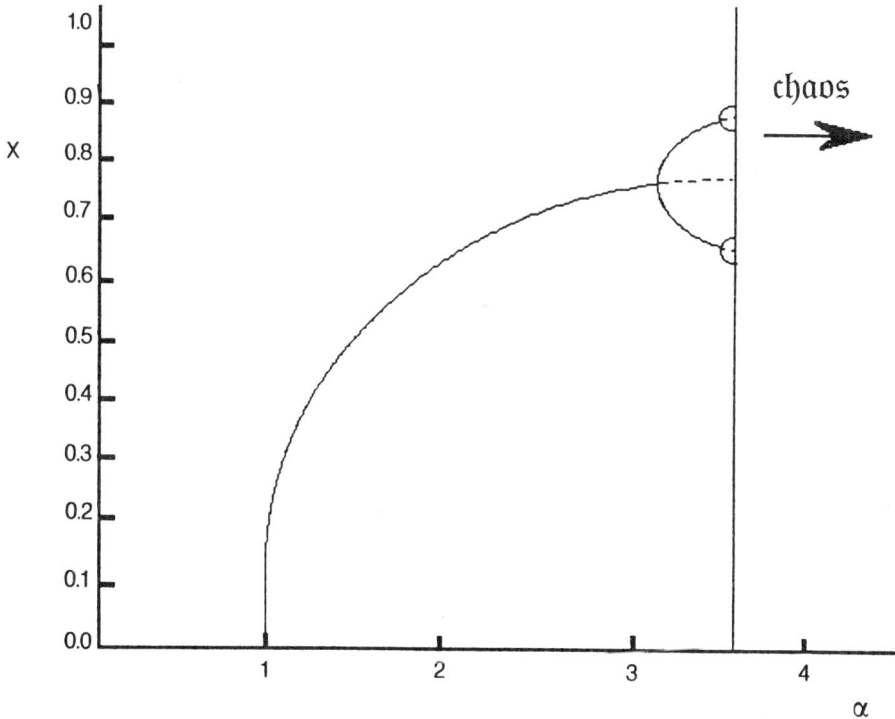

Diagram 1. First two Bifurcations of the Logistics Function $x_t = \alpha x_{t-1}(1 - x_{t-1})$

The diagram indicates the location of equilibrium points x_t as a function of the parameter α for $\alpha \geq 1$; a solid line indicates a stable equilibrium and a dashed line an unstable one. From $\alpha = 1$ to about $\alpha = 3.24$, there is only one stable equilibrium, but at this value of α the equilibrium splits (bifurcates) into two new stable equilibrium and one unstable one. Then, at about $\alpha = 3.54$, each of the stable equilibria again splits. Only the first two bifurcations are shown, but higher order ones occur at values of α greater than 3.54 but less than 3.57. Indeed, the higher order bifurcations occur at values of α following a simple convergent geometrical progression, with the parameter of the progression being equal to Feigenbaum's constant $\delta (\approx 4.6692)$. At the point of accumulation of this progression (at $\alpha \approx 3.57$) there are no further bifurcations, and above this value of α the process becomes chaotic.

In an economic phenomenon, however, the process underlying the phenomenon is unlikely ever to become chaotic, or at least not for processes generating clusters of economic activity. As chaos of economic activity. As chaos is approached, the number of stable equilibria increases without bound, an unlikely result in a real economy. A necessary (but not sufficient) condition for there actually to be chaos is that the unstable equilibria be dense in the chaotic region of the phase space, i.e., that in any subregion of this phase space, even a very small subregion, there be a countable infinity of unstable equilibria; again, this is a condition that would be highly unrealistic in a real economy.

Perhaps more to the point, in the real world, frictional costs will also typically prevent old clusters of activity from disappearing altogether. In the formal models it is assumed that factors are clustered on a single point and move from an old equilibrium to a new one costlessly, whereas in real life there will be substantial costs associated with the physical movement of capital and labor that will tend to keep them in place. Indeed, these adjustment costs give an existing cluster some incumbency advantage.

Nonetheless, the models suggest that changing circumstances can cause the incumbency advantages of established clusters to erode such that, over time, new clusters of an activity arise and the importance of an old cluster declines. The theory predicts that, if the critical parameter grows linearly, the bifurcations (new clusters) will occur increasingly rapidly.[20]

What is the reason for bifurcations – the creation of new clusters of economic activity for which incumbent clusters already exist – from an economic perspective? If, as has been posited throughout this exposition, the cluster is based on the existence of a localized external economy of scale, then new clusters will occur when the demand for the end product produced within the cluster grows to the point where more than one cluster can be economically sustained. This would occur, e.g., if cost curves of producers in the cluster were to reach a horizontal asymptote. But, even if scale economies persist, costs cannot decline at a constant rate forever as scale is increased. Indeed, costs must eventually behave asymptotically even if they approach zero; otherwise, costs would eventually become negative, an impossibility.[21] As costs of producers in an existing cluster approach the minimum (even if asymptotically), there is little further economy to be achieved in expanding output at that cluster, and as demand continues to increase, logistical costs will eventually drive producers to create a new cluster in some location apart from the original cluster.

Of course, if a point of maximum scale economy is reached such that output above that scale is subject to rising average costs, then it is clear that at some level of demand it would also be economical for one cluster to split into two.

The main point to be had from this discussion is that in economic geography models, the optimal location(s) of production shifts (shift) in response to demand increases rather than in response to changes in relative factor costs associated with the locations. However, once a cluster of activity is created, incumbency advantages will cause that cluster to continue to exist even if, in the face of

---

[20] The reader is reminded that a linear growth process implies that the rate of growth is continuously *decreasing*.

[21] These remarks are predicated on the notion that, subject to the external scale economy, average cost always declines with respect to output. The asymptotic nature of the costs is simply a reflection of the fact that eventually they must begin to decline at continuously decreasing rates if costs are not to fall belowzero.

increasing demand, it ceases to be the theoretically optimum location (or among the theoretic optima).

Importantly for this discussion, changing advantages associated with a location do not necessarily imply changing advantages associated with ownership. One implication is that the OLI paradigm can be married to the new economic geography theory. In particular, if there results a change in the optimal location of a cluster of economic activity but no change in ownership and internalization advantages held by one or several firms, one might expect these to shift their operations from the old to the new location or, at least, to concentrate new additions to capacity at the new location. Such a shift in the location of a firm's operations to a change in locational advantage is, for example, envisaged by Dunning 1991, but he ascribes the shift to changes in relative factor prices (i.e., shifts in comparative advantage along HOS lines) without dealing with exactly why comparative advantage might shift from one place on the map to another in the first place. And, indeed, given that so much of FDI flows from advanced nations to other advanced nations in which relative factor costs are not likely to be greatly different, it is difficult to see how this FDI could be driven by changing configurations of factor prices. Economic geography theory as an explanator of FDI thus holds a major advantage over Dunning's approach, in that the former theory needs no recourse to (often implausible) shifts in classical comparative advantage to motivate it.

This is because, if a national boundary separates the old cluster from the new one, direct investment can be driven by demand growth – i.e., exactly the same force that causes the new cluster of economic activity to arise, if the resulting shift in L advantage is independent of shifts in O and I advantages. This line of reasoning would appear to be especially suited to explaining horizontal direct investment within Europe or other regions (e.g., North America, East Asia).

The bifurcation considered above is one where two clusters of essentially identical economic activity arise as the result of the splitting of activities formerly done in just one cluster. This implies that all operations in the vertical chain of production are performed in both locations. However, it is not out of the question that the bifurcation will affect only certain stages of the vertical production chain, e.g., that downstream operations undergo bifurcation but upstream operations remain clustered at the original site. Thus, bifurcation can result in partial geographic separation of vertical operations. The remarks noted above about trade effects of such separation (i.e., that it creates two way trade) may in this context need some modification, e.g., if the bifurcation involves downstream operations, the trade effect may be that export of finished goods from the original site is replaced by export of intermediate goods. Because the bifurcation is driven by market growth, the total value of exports of the original location might growth even though the unit value of exports would decline.

5 Some Concluding Remarks

The above remarks (in sections 2 and through 4) should make it abundantly clear that when it comes to foreign direct investment and the multinational enterprise, our understanding is far from complete. Some areas of future research that are suggested by these remarks include:

(1) Modernization of the models of FDI based on firm rivalry. The models discussed in the third section of this paper are to modern industrial economics about as the original IBM personal computer is to the new pentium-driven machines: more than ten years behind the times. The models depend upon overly simplistic assumptions, often implicit ones, e.g., of complete information and constant returns to scale. Many advances have been made in the treatment of incomplete information or information that is asymmetrically shared by rivals, and these should be incorporated into the FDI models. Likewise, the effort should be made to incorporate increasing returns to scale, uncertain demand, and other features that might make the models accord better with reality.

(2) Further development of the determinants of "L" advantages. The previous section of this paper describes what is becoming a new frontier in economic research, the relationships between "thick market" externalities and the location of economic activity. It is clear (to this author at least!) that there is much promise to this approach, if only because so many questions remain unanswered. What determines where and when clusters form? What role do factors exogenous to the models (e.g., education, provision of infrastructure) play in this formation and the determination of exactly what types of economic activity are located there? What are the dynamics of a cluster (e.g., what parameters affect the bifurcation process)?

These last are exciting issues that bear upon fundamental questions of the times, such as how and why certain nations (or regions, or metropolitan areas) become prosperous and others don't, as well as upon why, how, and where foreign direct investment occurs. Indeed, direct investment and the presence of multinational enterprise seems to be increasingly linked to the overall well being of an area. But, even after thirty five years of research on MNEs, the relationships between MNEs and the wealth of nations are not well established. Thus, one can anticipate that foreign direct investment and the multinational enterprise will remain an exciting area of research for some time to come.

Bibliography

Acocella N (1992) Strategic Foreign Investment in the EC. In: Cantwell J (ed) Multinational Investment and Modern Europe: Strategic Interaction in the Integrated Community. Edward Elgar, Aldershot

Baer HL jr (1984) Competition among the Multinationals: Examination of Equilibrium in Multimarket Oligopolies. Northwestern University Economics Department Ph.D. Dissertation, Evanston, Illinois

Brander J, Krugman PR (1983) A Reciprocal Dumping Model of International Trade. Journal of International Economics 15:313–321

Blomström M, Lipsey RE, Kulchyck K (1988) US and Swedish Direct Investment and Exports. In: Baldwin RE (ed) Trade Policy Issues and Empirical Analysis. University of Chicago Press, for the National Bureau of Economic Research, Chicago

Buckley PJ, Casson MC (1976) The Future of the Multinational Enterprise. MacMillan, London

Buigues P, Jacquemin A (1994) Foreign Direct Investment and Exports to the European Community. In: Mason M, Encarnation D (eds) Does Ownership Matter: Japanese Multinationals in Europe. The Oxford University Press, Oxford New York

Cantwell J (1990) The Technological Competency Theory of International Production and its Implications. University of Reading Discussion Papers in International Investment and Business Studies, Serie B, 3, 149

Casson MC (1991) Economic Theories of International Business: A Research Agenda. Working paper, Department of Economics, Reading University

Coase RH (1937) The Nature of the Firm. Economica (New Series) 4:386–405

Corley TAB (1994) Britain's Overseas Investments in 1914 Revisited. Business History 36:71–88

Devaney RL (1989) An Introduction to Chaotic Dynamical Systems. Addison Wesley, Redwood City, CA

Dunning JH (1958) American Investment in British Industry. George Allen and Unwin, London

Dunning JH (1980) Towards an Eclectic Theory of International Production: Some Empirical Tests. Journal of International Business Studies 11/1:9–31

Dunning JH (1988) Explaining International Production. Allen and Unwin, London

Dunning JH (1991) The Eclectic Paradigm of International Production: A Personal Perspective. In: Pitelis, Sugden (eds) The Nature of the Transnational Firm. Routledge, London

Dunning JH (1993) Multinational Enterprise and the Global Economy. Addison Wesley, Wokingham, England

Dunning JH (1994) Explaining Foreign Direct Investment in Japan: Some Theoretical Insights. Paper presented at the Wharton School, University of Pennsylvania, October 7

Flowers EB (1976) Oligopolistic Reactions in European and Canadian Direct Investment in the United States. Journal of International Business Studies 7:43–55

Fudenberg D, Maskin E: The Folk Theorem in Repeated Games with Discounting or with Incomplete Information. Econometrica 54/3:533–554

Gleick JC (1987) Chaos. Penguin Books, London

Graham EM (1978) Transatlantic Investment by Multinational Firms: A Rivalistic Phenomenon?. Journal of Post Keynesian Economics 1:82–99

Graham EM (1990) Exchange of Threat Between Multinational Firms as an Infinitely Repeated Noncooperative Game. The International Trade Journal 4:259–278

Graham EM (1994) US Direct Investment Abroad and US Exports in the Manufacturing Sector: Some Empirical Results Based on Cross Sectional Analysis. Paper presented at colloquium held at La Sorbonne, June 6–8

Hymer SH (1959) The International Operations of National Firms: A Study of Direct Foreign Investment. MIT Department of Economics Doctoral Dissertation, Cambridge, Mass.; printed at The MIT Press, Cambridge, Massachusetts 1976

Hymer SH, Bowthorne R (1970) Multinational Corporations and International Oligopoly: The Non American Challenge. In: Kindleberger CP (ed) The International Corporation. The MIT Press, Cambridge, Massachusetts

Jones G (1994) The Making of Global Enterprise. Business History 36:1–17

Julius DA (1991) Foreign Direct Investment: The Neglected Twin of Trade. The Group of 30, Occasional Paper No. 33, Washington DC

Katseli L (1991) Foreign Direct Investment and Trade Interlinkages in the 1990s: Experience and Prospects of Developing Countries. Paper prepared for UNCTC/UNCTAD project on The New Globalism and Developing Countries: Investment, Trade, and Technology Linkages in the 1990s

Krugman PR (1991) Geography and Trade. The MIT Press, Cambridge, Mass

Lipsey RE, Weiss MY (1981) Foreign Production and Exports in Manufacturing Industries. Review of Economics and Statistics 63:488–494

Lipsey RE, Weiss MY (1984) Foreign Production and Exports of Individual Firms. Review of Economics and Statistics 66:304–308

Mundell RA (1957) International Trade and Factor Mobility. American Economic Review 47:321–335

Onida F (1989) Multinational Firms, International Competition, and Oligopolistic Rivalry: Theoretical Trends. Revista di Politica Economica 79 (3rd Series): 79–138

Penrose ET (1956) Foreign Investment and the Growth of the Firm. Economic Journal 66:220–235

Porter M (1990) The Competitive Advantage of Nations. The Free Press, New York

Sanna-Randaccio F (1990) European Direct Investment in US Manufacturing. Edizioni Kappa, Rome

Vernon R (1966) International Investment and International Trade in the Product Cycle. Quarterly Journal of Economics 83/1:190–207

Vernon R (1974) The Location of Economic Activity. In: Dunning J (ed) Economic Analysis and the Multinational Enterprise. George Allen and Unwin, London

Wells LT (1972) The Product Life Cycle and International Trade. The Harvard Graduate School of Business, Division of Research, Boston, Massachusetts

Wilkins M (1994) Comparative Hosts. Business History 36:18–50

Williamson OE (1970) Corporate Control and Business Behavior. Prentice Hall, Engelwood Cliffs

Williamson OE (1973) Markets and Hierarchies: Some Elementary Considerations. American Economic Review 61:316–325

Yu C-M, Kiyohiko I (1988) Oligopolistic Reaction and Foreign Direct Investment: The Case of the US Tire and Textile Industries. Journal of International Business Studies 19:449–460